THANK YOU FOR
FLYING WITH US

Other ESP titles of interest include:

ADAMSON, D.
*International Hotel English**

BINHAM, P. *et al.*
*Hotel English**

BINHAM, P. *et al.*
*Restaurant English**

BLAKEY, T.
*English for Maritime Studies (second edition)**

BRIEGER, N. and J. COMFORT
*Business Contacts**

BRIEGER, N. and J. COMFORT
Business Issues

BRIEGER, N. and J. COMFORT
*Early Business Contacts**

BRIEGER, N. and J. COMFORT
*Social Contacts**

BRIEGER, N. and J. COMFORT
*Technical Contacts**

BRIEGER, N. and A. CORNISH
*Secretarial Contacts**

DAVIES, S. *et al.*
Bilingual Handbooks of Business Correspondence and Communication

KEANE, L.
*International Restaurant English**

McGOVERN, J. and J. McGOVERN
*Bank on Your English**

PALSTRA, R.
*Telephone English**

PALSTRA, R.
Telex English

POTE, M. *et al.*
*A Case for Business English**

ROBERTSON, F.
*Airspeak**

* includes audio cassette(s)

THANK YOU FOR FLYING WITH US
English for In-Flight Cabin Attendants

JOHN G. BEECH
Air Service Training Limited, Perth, Scotland

Longman

Pearson Education Limited,
Edinburgh Gate, Harlow
Essex CM20 2JE, England
and Associated Companies throughout the World

www.longman-elt.com

First Published 1990 by Prentice Hall International (UK) Ltd
This edition published by Pearson Education Ltd 2000
Third impression 2000

© International Book Distributors Ltd

All rights reserved. No reproduction, copy or transmission
of this publication may be made without written permission
or in accordance with the provisions of the Copyright, Designs
and Patents Act 1988, or under the terms of any licence
permitting limited copying issued by the Copyright Licensing
Agency, 90 Tottenham Court Road, London, W1P 9HE.

Typeset in $10\frac{1}{2}/12$ pt Palacio
by MHL Typesetting Ltd, Coventry

Printed and bound in Malaysia, LSP

Library of Congress Cataloging-in-Publication Data

Beech, John G. 1947–
    Thank you for flying with us: English for in-flight cabin attendants/John G. Beech.
    p. cm.
    ISBN 0-13-912635-X: $10.95
    1. English language — Conversation and phrase books (for flight attendants). 2. English language — Textbooks for foreign speakers. I. Title.
PE1116.F55B44 1990
428.3′4′0243877—dc20

British Library Cataloguing in Publication Data

Beech, John G. (John Greatrex) 1947–
    Thank you for flying with us: English for in-flight cabin attendants.
    1. Language. Spoken English
    I. title
    428.3

ISBN 0-13-912635-X

CONTENTS

Acknowledgements — viii

INTRODUCTION — 1

SELF ASSESSMENT — 3

Unit 1 THE FLIGHT CREW — 4
The Crew 4; The Role of the Cabin Crew 8;
Useful Words and Phrases Summary 9

Unit 2 BOARDING — 10
The Captain's Briefing 10; Crew Duties (1) 13; Crew Duties (2) 15; Departure Lounge Announcements 18; Boarding the Aircraft 19; Seat Allocation (1) 20; Seat Allocation (2) 22; Stowage of Baggage 25; Welcome Announcement 26; Safety Announcements and Demonstrations 28; Life Jackets 29;
Useful Words and Phrases Summary 32

Unit 3 TAKE-OFF AND INITIAL FLIGHT — 33
Ramp Duties 33; Take-off Procedures 36;
Useful Words and Phrases Summary 38

Unit 4 FOOD AND DRINK — 39
Meals 39; Silver Service 45; Complaints 46; Drinks Service 48; Equipment 52;
Useful Words and Phrases Summary 53

Unit 5 IN-FLIGHT ENTERTAINMENT — 54
Movies/Films 54; Passenger Arm-Rest Controls 57; Passenger Service Units 58; Passengers' Reading Material 59;
Useful Words and Phrases Summary 60

Unit 6 DUTY-FREE SALES — 61
Preliminary Announcements 61; Duty-Free Allowances 64;
Useful Words and Phrases Summary 65

Unit 7 GENERAL PASSENGER QUERIES AND PROBLEMS — 66
Technical 66; Destination Information 68; Time Changes 69; Nursing Mothers 71; Miscellaneous 72; Passengers' Complaints 75; Dealing with Problems and Queries 76;
Useful Words and Phrases Summary 77

Unit 8 EMERGENCY PROCEDURES — 78
Cabin Depressurisation 78; Forced Landing 80; Emergency Procedure Announcements 84;
Useful Words and Phrases Summary 87

Unit 9 FIRST AID — 88
Medical Supplies 88; The Body 89; Initial Enquiries 91; Getting to Know the Illnesses 93

Unit 10 ADDITIONAL ANNOUNCEMENTS — 95
Delays 95; Aborted Departure 97; Turbulence Announcement 98; Passenger Identification Announcement 98; Diversion Announcement 99; Landing Card Announcement 99; Delayed Landing Announcement 101;
Useful Words and Phrases Summary 101

Unit 11 LANDING, TRANSIT AND DISEMBARKATION — 102
Descent 102; Descent Announcement 102; Final Approach 103; After-Landing Announcement 103;

Contents vii

Transit Variations 104; Taxying and Disembarkation 105; Useful Words and Phrases Summary 106

Appendix A **FINAL TEST** **107**

Appendix B **GETTING A JOB AS A CA** **112**

TAPESCRIPT **113**

GLOSSARY **124**

ACKNOWLEDGEMENTS

I was given considerable help and advice in the finalisation of this book and I would particularly like to thank the following individuals: Hugh Beech, Claudine Bellegarde-Deakin, Gradimir Dunčić, Peter McDougall, Barbara Sabatini, Ian Walker and Maggie Yerolatsitis. Thanks are also due to my colleagues Mike McGrath and Billie Beech, who have influenced my approach to ESP over many years. Billie, my wife, must also be thanked for her considerable patience while I was working on this book. Finally, I would like to thank Pauline Young and Shona Fellowes for typing the script.

The following organisations have been generous in providing materials for illustrations:

Airbus Industrie
Air France
Air UK
Boeing
British Aerospace
British Airways
EECO
Fokker
Gulf Air
Henshalls
HM Immigration
JAT
L.A. Rumbold
Lufthansa
McDonnell Douglas
PTC Aerospace
Rauette Limited & Joel Rothman
Royal Brunei Airlines
Short Bros.
Singapore Airlines
Steels Aviation Services
Swissair

The test draws on the highly successful ARELS Examinations Trust format for exams in Spoken English, which I have marked for a number of years, and due acknowledgement is freely given.

INTRODUCTION

The book

This book has been designed, in so far as it is possible, to meet the needs of both class study and individual study. All material is suitable for class use and, with the clear exception of the test, the individual student should be able to work through the book finding that all necessary items are explained or included in the Glossary. However, as much of the work of a cabin attendant involves interaction with passengers, many exercises are based on role play and/or pair work.

The cassette

The cassette contains all the material used for listening purposes. This consists of announcements, statements and passengers' comments and questions — in a variety of accents — for repetition, information retrieval, comprehension and response. These items are indicated by the symbol ⊙⊙.

The test

The test should be entirely spoken. The major parts test ability to make announcements and the necessary skills for interaction with passengers. It should be conducted by a qualified and experienced EFL teacher, and, ideally but not necessarily, in a language laboratory. A trial run is recommended to practise the pausing of the test tape to allow gaps for students' answers.

Usage

English is not entirely standardised in the international world of the cabin attendant. For example, the term 'cabin attendant' is British English, the American English equivalent being 'flight attendant'. Throughout this book the British English term is used.

In other cases, both American and British terms are used, to reflect more the reality of the lingua franca of the cabin crew. With regard to general usage, British English is used throughout, except in some passenger roles. However, when there are differences between British and American spellings of place names, the American spelling has been adopted. This reflects the dominant status of American English in manuals for ground services passenger handling.

Throughout this book, 'he' and 'she' are entirely interchangeable, and apologies are offered for any inferred, but not implied, sexism. The old stereotypes of male passengers and female cabin crew are an absurdity in today's world.

The methodology

This course adopts an eclectic approach. The texts are as authentic as possible and the exercises vary. They have one thing in common: they are designed to make students practise the linguistic skills which they will actually need during the course of their work. Any emphasis on structure, on functions, on repetition, on comprehension or on sentence reformulation, for example, is only made when it is appropriate to real-life circumstances. The underlying objectives throughout the course are to familiarise students with procedures and terminology in English and with passengers' use of many different varieties of English, and to assist them in responding appropriately and accurately.

Some words of caution

Aviation is an industry which is both heavily legislated and ever-changing. Any information in this book is thus only given for language-training purposes. This caveat applies across the whole range of material from, for example, the details of safety equipment and procedures to prices in the BA bar tariff.

Names of real airlines etc. have been used throughout, with the exception of some film examples, to avoid the hollow ring that concocted names often have. This does not imply that a particular airline uses a particular announcement as given in the text, or that its tacit approval is carried.

Airline names, airport names and flight numbers can, of course, be varied when practising announcements.

SELF ASSESSMENT

Think about the different ways you use your own language in different situations. For example, is the way you speak with your friends the same as the way you should speak to passengers?

Now consider your general level of English. Mark one of the boxes.

Beginner ⟶ Elementary ⟶ Intermediate ⟶ Advanced

For the next section you may need help as it is difficult to judge your own levels of spoken English: on a scale of 0 to 10 mark yourself in these particular skills.

Pronunciation   _____
Fluency   _____
Accuracy   _____
Naturalness   _____
Formality   _____

Finally, give a mark for your knowledge of the English which is specific to cabin crew.   _____

Check

Do you know the meaning of the following words in the context of air travel?

| airbridge | aisle | apron | to brief | CIP | PAX |
| to ditch | galley | to stow | trolley | UM | brace for impact |

Perhaps you want to change your last mark!

Now, decide objectives for improving your different skills. Discuss these with your teacher if you are not working alone.

UNIT 1

THE FLIGHT CREW

Can you name the job of each member of this flight crew?

THE CREW

Reading

Read the following text and answer the questions

The men and women who work in an aircraft when it is flying from one city to another are called the flight crew. They can be divided into two groups: those who fly the aircraft and those who work with the passengers.

The Flight Crew

The first group consists normally of two people, who work on the flight deck. The more senior is the pilot who is called the captain. There is a second pilot, known as the co-pilot. The co-pilot may hold the same rank as the captain or he may hold the lower rank of First Officer. One some airliners there is a flight engineer who is responsible for monitoring the airliner's engines and systems. More and more this responsibility is being taken over by the two pilots, and two-man crews are common.

The people who work in the cabin with the passengers are called the cabin crew, and this book is designed for them. The senior member of the cabin crew, who is responsible to the captain, is called the flight director or cabin services director on wide-bodied aircraft, the Boeing 747, for example, and the purser on smaller aircraft. On wide-bodied aircraft, a purser is in charge of a separate cabin area or class of passengers, and reports to the flight director or cabin services director.

Those who work under the senior member of the cabin crew are called stewards or stewardesses (or air hostesses) by the public, but they should be correctly called cabin attendants, or CAs for short.

The minimum number of cabin attendants working on a particular flight is determined by the number of passengers and/or the aircraft type and its number of emergency exits. If there are a large number of children travelling alone, extra CAs are used.

No. of passengers	Minimum no. of cabin attendants
20–50	1
51–100	2
101–150	3
151–200	4
201 Plus	4 +1 for every additional 25 passengers

The figures are those recommended by the International Civil Aviation Organisation (ICAO). Regulations in each particular country apply to aircraft registered in that country.

The maximum number of CAs is determined by the airline, and it depends on the level of service required.

1 *How many cabin attendants are required by ICAO on the following flights, remembering that this is determined by the number of passengers and not the number of seats?*

Aircraft type	No. of seats	Load factor*	No. of cabin attendants
Airbus A320	179	65	
ATR 42	74	89	
Boeing 727	189	81	
Boeing 737	149	58	
Boeing 747	660	82	
Boeing 757	239	83	
Boeing 767	220	92	
BAe ATP	64	85	
CASA 212	26	81	
Dornier 228	19	100	
Embraer Bandeirante	19	84	
Fokker F.27	44	48	
L-1011 (Tristar)	400	89	
MD-80	172	79	
MD-11	405	65	

The numbers of seats given above refer to particular configurations of seats.

* The load factor is the percentage of seats occupied.

The Flight Crew

2

(a) What is the name of the group of people who work on an airliner?

_____

(b) Who is the most senior person on an airliner?

_____

(c) Who does he share his work with?

_____

(d) What are the two ranks that pilots hold?

_____

(e) Where do pilots work?

_____

(f) Who is sometimes the third member of the flight deck team?

_____

(g) Who is the senior member of the cabin crew?

_____

(h) What is the correct name for a member of the cabin crew?

_____

Language practice

Fill in the blanks in the following sentences

(a) The flight crew consists _____ two groups of people.
(b) The co-pilot may hold the same rank _____ the captain.
(c) A flight engineer is responsible _____ monitoring the aircraft's engines.
(d) This responsibility is being taken _____ by the pilots.
(e) The purser is responsible _____ the captain.
(f) Cabin attendants are called CAs _____ short.
(g) The minimum numbers of CAs may be determined _____ the number of passengers.
(h) Regulations in a particular country apply _____ aircraft registered in that country.

THE ROLE OF THE CABIN CREW

Reading

Read the following text

It must always be remembered that cabin attendants are required by law to work on an airliner for reasons of safety. As well as their obvious role in an emergency, they have routine responsibilities for safety. They must ensure that passengers fasten their seatbelts and do not smoke, as required by the captain. Cabin attendants must watch out for any behaviour by passengers such as drunkenness which might cause a dangerous situation.

The cabin attendant is the member of the airline's staff who has the most contact with the public. The passengers' impression of the airline will depend largely upon how well the cabin attendants do their job. It is for this reason that both the training and the performance of the cabin attendants are so important. In the handling of passengers, or PAX as they are termed in the airline industry, language is important at two levels.

You must be able to communicate with the passenger. This will be no problem if you share the same mother-tongue. If you do not, English will probably be the means of communication. The English you have learned at school will help, but you may need more practice in spoken English.

Being able to communciate with a passenger is, however, not enough for a cabin attendant. So, secondly, your language level must be high enough to show:

(a) professionalism
(b) politeness
(c) respectfulness

You may need English to report a cabin fault at a foreign airport. Many airliners are built in English-speaking countries and you may want to refer to the manufacturer's manual. Finally, in some countries, you may find that training is given in English.

It is the aim of this book to help your English in these ways.

The Flight Crew

Useful words and phrases summary

crew
captain
flight deck
purser
cabin attendant (CA)
ICAO
emergency
responsibility
PAX
cabin services manager
rank

wide-bodied aircraft
consist of
same rank as
higher/lower rank than
responsible for (+ing)
in charge of
report to
fasten seatbelts
watch out for
refer to

UNIT 2

BOARDING

*Where do you think these people are?
What do you think is happening?*

THE CAPTAIN'S BRIEFING

Reading

Read the following text and answer the questions.

The start of a flight for the crew takes place in the Operations Room of the airport. The captain collects the available information, particularly the weather conditions, and files his flight plan. He is told any important information about the passengers. He and the cabin services manager then brief the crew.

For cabin attendants, there are two particular points that they should note. Firstly, if weather conditions are bad, the flight may be delayed or even diverted. In this case the CAs must be ready to deal with passengers for whom this creates a problem. In less severe conditions, the flight may take place on schedule, but turbulence may cause problems for the cabin attendants as they work, and passengers may need reassuring.

Secondly, cabin attendants must note if any important passengers are booked on the flight. They may be VIPs (very important persons), such as politicians, religious leaders and people famous in the worlds of sport and entertainment, or CIPs (commercially important persons) such as executives of other airlines. Religious leaders and aristocrats may need a special form of address. As well as looking after such passengers with particular care and courtesy, it may be appropriate to make a special announcement during the flight. For example, some airlines have a policy of announcing congratulations to winning sports teams.

The purser will brief the cabin crew of any special requirements that passengers may have. This may include special meals, for religious or health reasons, and special seating arrangements for disabled or ill passengers. Such passengers as unaccompanied minors (UMs) are normally pre-boarded; that is, they board the aircraft before the main group of passengers. Cabin attendants need to be especially attentive with UMs as the airline has accepted responsibility for their travel.

Which of the following statements are true? How can you change the false ones to make them true?

(a) The purser collects all the necessary information for the flight.

(b) The captain is told about any special passengers.

(c) There are two pieces of information that CAs should listen for during the briefing.

(d) Passengers need to be comforted when there is turbulence.

(e) VIPs are very immature persons.

(f) CIPs are people who are important to the airline for business reasons.

(g) All passengers must be looked after courteously.

(h) The captain briefs CAs on any particular needs of passengers.

(i) A UM is a child travelling alone.

(j) UMs are always put on the aircraft before the other passengers.

Listening 1 🔊

Listen to the information on the tape. Complete the table below. In particular, imagine that you are Sandra and take note of any specific duties.

Destination	
Aircraft type	
Flight time	
Meal service	
Seating/classes	
Crew/duty area	
CIP/VIP/UM etc.	
Special meals	
Language for announcements	

Boarding

CREW DUTIES (1)

Reading

Read the following text and do the exercise.

Following the captain's briefing in the Operations Room, the crew board the aircraft before the passengers: The cabin crew have a number of duties to perform both before the passengers board and during boarding.

Before the passengers arrive, the CAs must check that certain items of aircraft equipment are present on board. These vary from aircraft type to aircraft type. All movable safety equipment must be checked, and this would normally include:

Equipment	Action
Drugs kit	Check that the seal is intact.
First aid kits	Check that they are present and complete.
Halon fire extinguishers	Check that the seals are intact and the extinguishers are not past the date of expiry for use.
Portable oxygen masks/smoke hoods	Check the level and check for airtightness.
Slides/chutes	Check the pressure of the operating system
Axes	Check the seal.
Megaphone	Check by squeezing trigger.

The list above is typical, but each airline operator has its own specific list.

Identify the items of equipment illustrated below and match them with the descriptions of use.

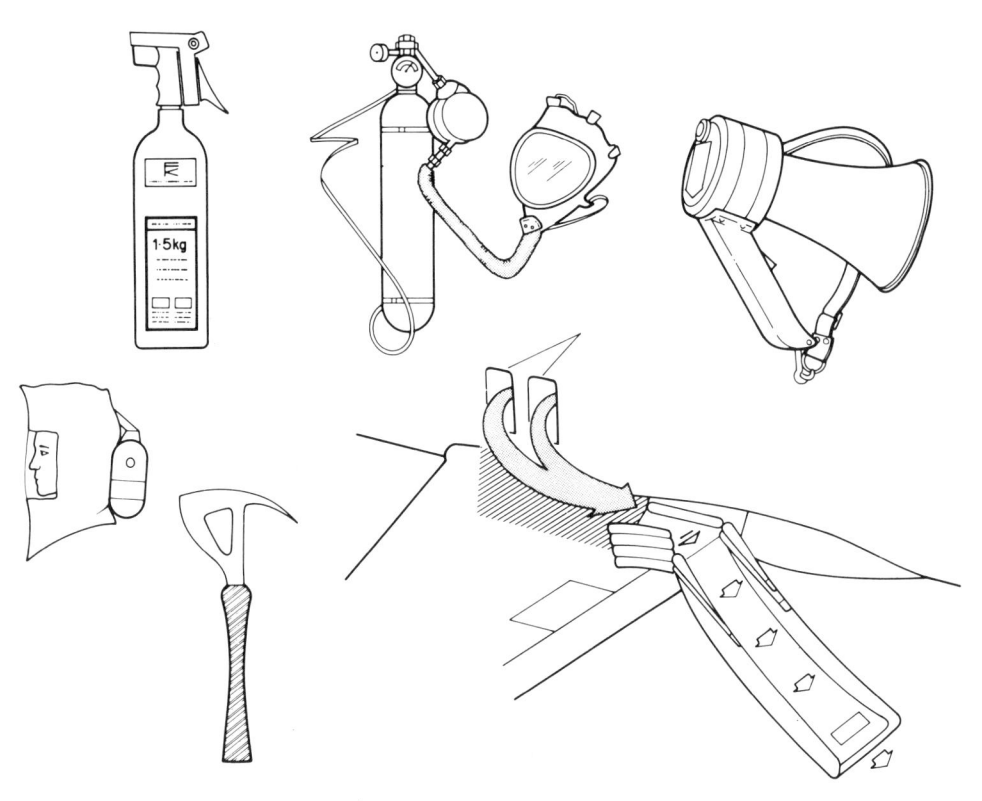

(a) It is used to speak to passengers in an emergency.

    _____

(b) They are used to fight fires.

    _____

(c) This provides oxygen in an emergency.

    _____

(d) You would use this for leaving the aircraft in an emergency.

    _____

(e) This would help you breathe in a fire.

    _____

(f) This can be used to break things in an emergency.

    _____

Boarding 15

CREW DUTIES (2)

Reading

Read the following text and do the exercises.

The cabin is divided into several areas for the purpose of pre-flight checks and the purser designates the CA responsible for each area. The CA then completes the check using a checklist. Both the public address (PA) system and the interphone may be used during these checks.

Here is a typical example of the location and distribution of equipment.

FORWARD ZONE

MOVABLE SAFETY EQUIPMENT

- FIRE AXE (1)
- CO_2 FIRE EXTINGUISHER (1)
- CREW LIFE VEST (2)
- SMOKE GOGGLES (4)
- ROPE (1)
- ROPE (1)
- CREW LIFE VEST (2)
- CREW MASK (5)
- O_2 BOTTLE (1)
- DRY CHEMICAL EXTINGUISHER (1)
- CA. LIFE VEST (2)

- (1) H_2O FIRE EXTINGUISHER
- (1) FIRST AID KIT
- (1) FIRE AXE
- (1) CA. LIFE VEST
- (1) ESCAPE SLIDE
- (2) LIFE RAFT
- (1) RADIO BEACON
- (1) MEGAPHONE
- (1) O_2 BOTTLE
- (1) CA. MASK
- (5) PASS. O_2 MASK
- (8) INFANT LIFE VEST
- (2) DEMO LIFE VEST
- (1) ESCAPE SLIDE

MID ZONE

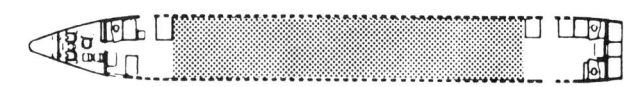

MOVABLE SAFETY EQUIPMENT

- ③ LIFE RAFT
- ④ ROPE
- PASS. LIFE VESTS

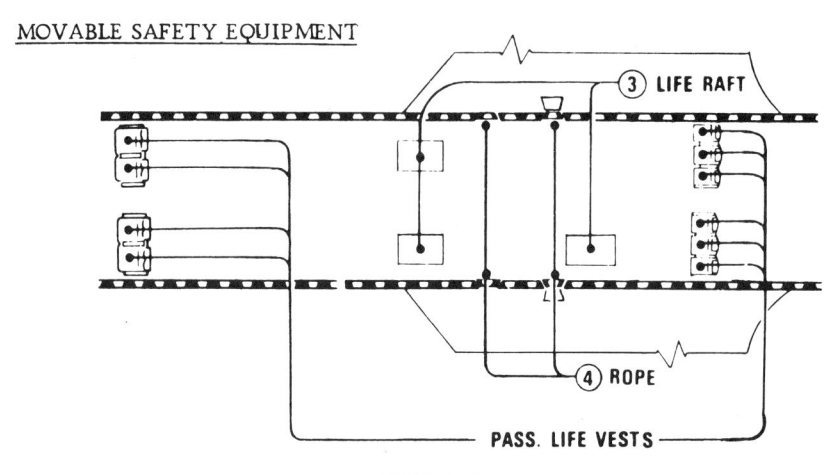

AFT ZONE

MOVABLE SAFETY EQUIPMENT

- ① DRY CHEMICAL EXTINGUISHER
- ① O₂ BOTTLE
- ① CA. MASK
- ⑥ PASS. O₂ MASK
- ② CA. LIFE VEST
- ② ESCAPE SLIDE
- ① FIRE AXE
- ② O₂ BOTTLE / CA. MASK
- ③ BABY COT
- ① MEGAPHONE
- ① FIRST AID KIT
- ① H₂O FIRE EXTINGUISHER
- ② CA. LIFE VEST

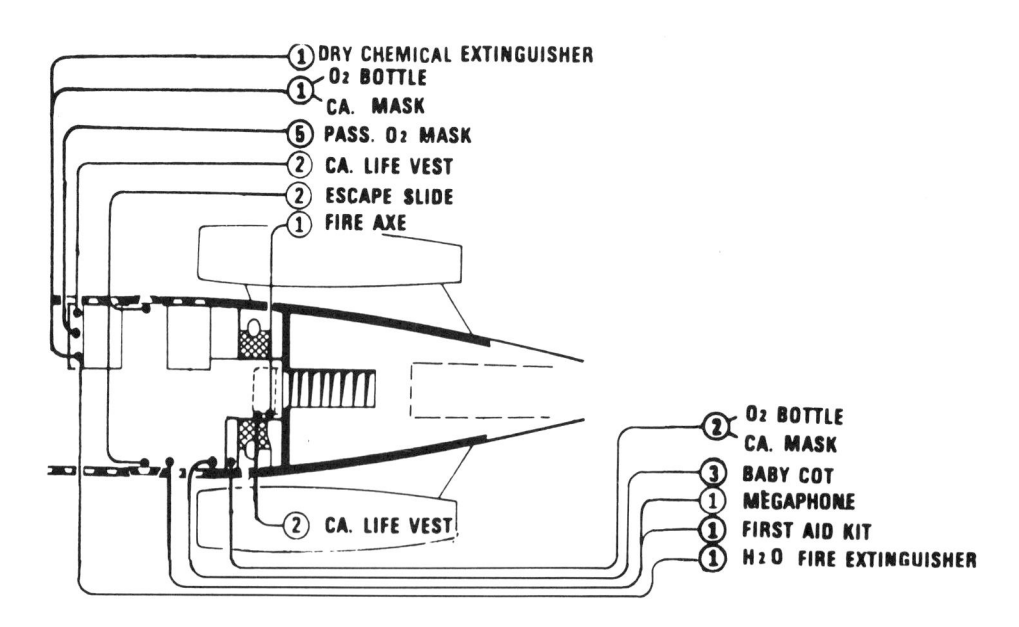

Boarding

The CAs have some general duties to perform before the passengers arrive. Doors and walking areas must be clear from obstruction. The position of the stairs or airbridge should be checked for safety. All food and drinks equipment and stores must be checked.

Once the passengers have boarded, the cabin crew must perform the duties, including the making of announcements, already given. Additionally, they must ensure that seats next to emergency exits are only occupied by able-bodied adults. A passenger head-count must be made for reasons of security.

The cabin crew are responsible for the closing of doors and must liaise with the captain, through the purser.

1 *Match each item of safety equipment in column A with its function in column B and a situation where it may be needed in column C. Draw lines to link the words. The first one is done for you.*

A Equipment	B Function	C Situation
Escape slide	to allow quick evacuation of aircraft	a forced landing on land or sea
Fire axe	to keep a person afloat in water	ditching in the sea
	to break a window or wall	a passenger cuts his hand on a broken glass
First aid kit	to put out an electrical fire	air crash on land
Dry chemical fire extinguisher		smoke is seen coming from an electrical socket
Life vest	to provide a number of things needed for illness or injury	

2 *Why do CAs have to check the following?*

(a) doors and walking areas
(b) seats next to emergency exits
(c) passengers

DEPARTURE LOUNGE ANNOUNCEMENTS

Listening 2

Normally ground services personnel announce the boarding of a flight from the departure lounge, and the first contact that the cabin attendants have with the passengers is when they actually board the aircraft.

However, in certain circumstances, it may be necessary for a cabin attendant to make the announcement over the PA system in the departure lounge.

Listen to the following model announcements and practise repeating the phrases.

1. Good morning, ladies and gentlemen.
   Aer Lingus flight no. EIN151 to Dublin is now ready for boarding. Passengers for this flight should proceed now through the door at the end of the departure lounge. Please extinguish all smoking material before leaving this lounge. Thank you.
2. Boarding will take place according to the seat numbers shown on the boarding cards. You are asked not to proceed through the gate until these numbers are called. Thank you.
3. Economy class passengers holding boarding cards with seat numbers between rows 15 and 25 are requested to board now. Thank you.

Language practice

Practise departure lounge announcements for the following flights, using the standard phrases heard in the model announcements:

Boarding

(a) Royal Jordanian   RJA 136 Amman
(b) UTA   UTA 808 Abidjan
(c) Aerolineas Argentinas   ARG 385 Buenos Aires
(d) Yugoslav Airlines   JAT 210 London
(e) Royal Brunei Airlines   RBI 430 Brunei Darussalam

BOARDING THE AIRCRAFT

Listening 3

Listen to the examples of cabin attendants exchanges with passengers boarding the aircraft, A to J, and match them with the following situations:

1. A man says he has never flown before.

2. A passenger drops her bag at the top of the steps and the contents fall out.

3. A young mother asks about feeding her baby.

4. A passenger lights a cigarette as he walks up the steps.

5. A young woman is crying as she enters the cabin.

6. A passenger requests reassurance about the flight and destination.

7. A passenger wants to know where to sit.

8. A female passenger smiles but says nothing on entering the cabin.

9. A passenger seems nervous and enquires how smooth the flight will be.

10. A passenger enquires about the duration of the flight.

Language practice

Practise welcoming passengers on board, in pairs. Students playing the role of passengers should invent some realistic things to say.

SEAT ALLOCATION (1)

Reading

Read the text opposite and answer the questions.

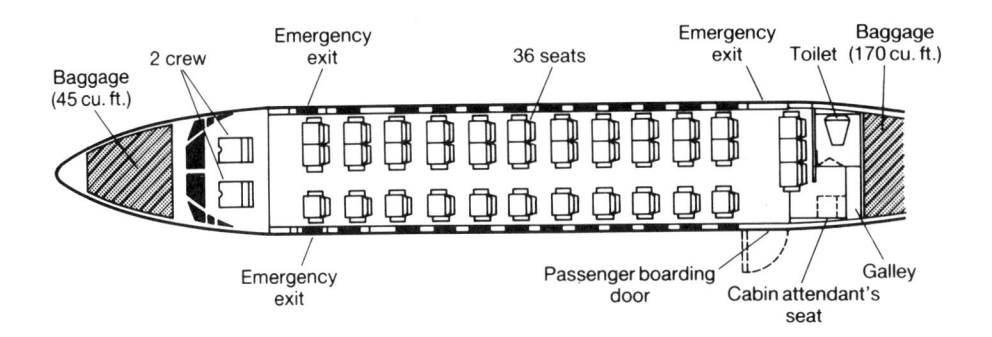

Labels on aircraft diagram:
- Baggage (45 cu. ft.)
- 2 crew
- Emergency exit
- 36 seats
- Emergency exit
- Toilet
- Baggage (170 cu. ft.)
- Emergency exit
- Passenger boarding door
- Cabin attendant's seat
- Galley

Single-class configuration on a Shorts 360–300.

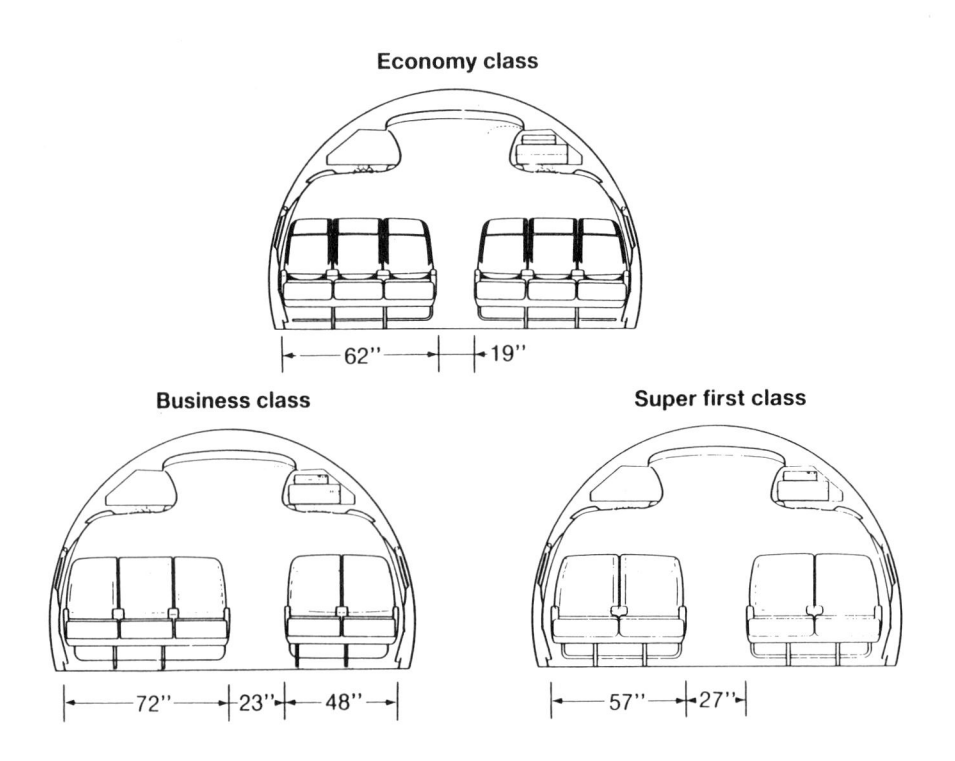

Economy class
62" 19"

Business class
72" 23" 48"

Super first class
57" 27"

Boarding 21

Flights carry one class only (known as economy or tourist), two classes (e.g. first and economy) or three classes. In the latter case, the extra class lies between first and economy and is known by different names to different airlines — business, executive, club, etc. First class is towards the nose of the aircraft and is generally separated from the other class(es) by a bulkhead with curtains. Each class can be distinguished by the size of the seats and the distance, or pitch, between them.

Two-class configuration on an Airbus A320.

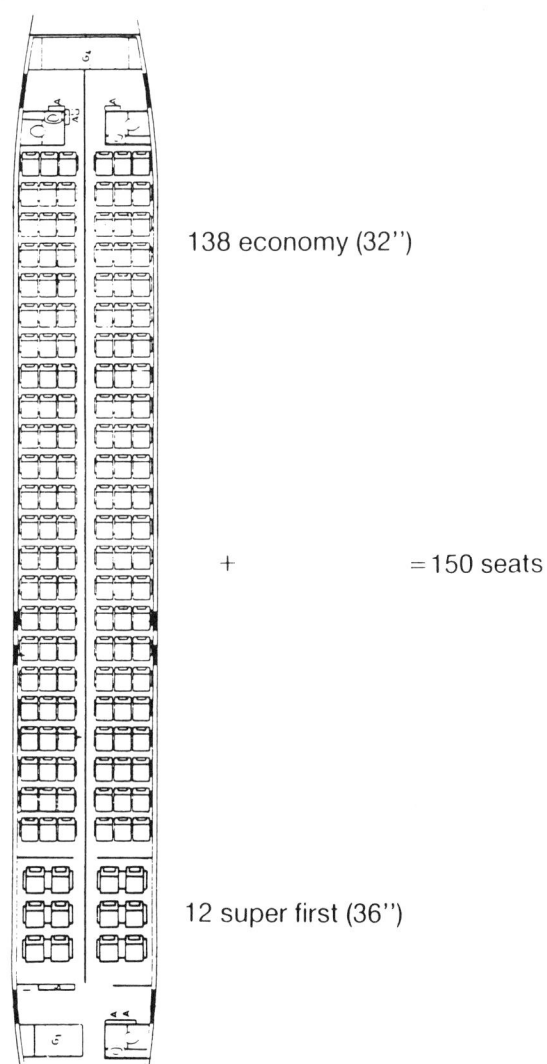

138 economy (32")

+

= 150 seats

12 super first (36")

1   Do all flights have more than one passenger class?
2   Name some passenger classes which are between first class and economy class.
3   In what ways are the seats different in each class?

SEAT ALLOCATION (2)

Reading

Read the following text and answer the questions.

On most flights seats are allocated to passengers at the check-in desk. The seat number is often recorded on the passenger's boarding pass:

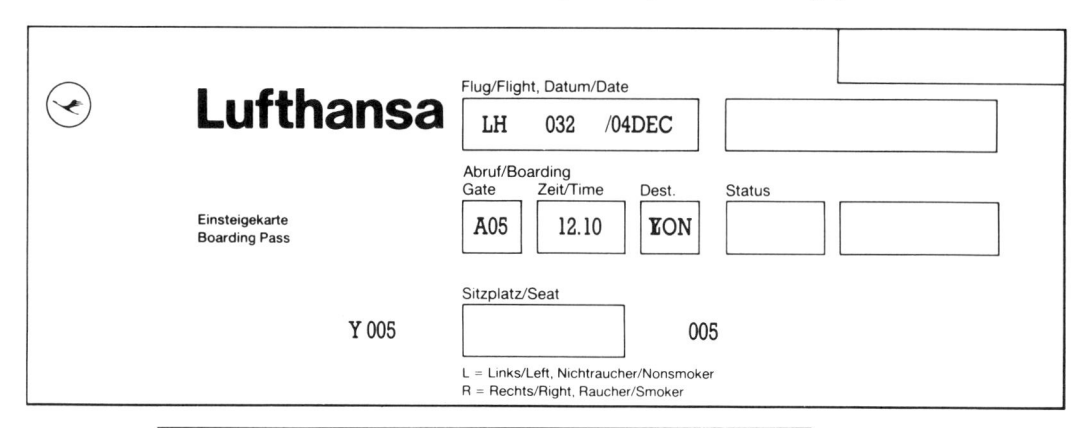

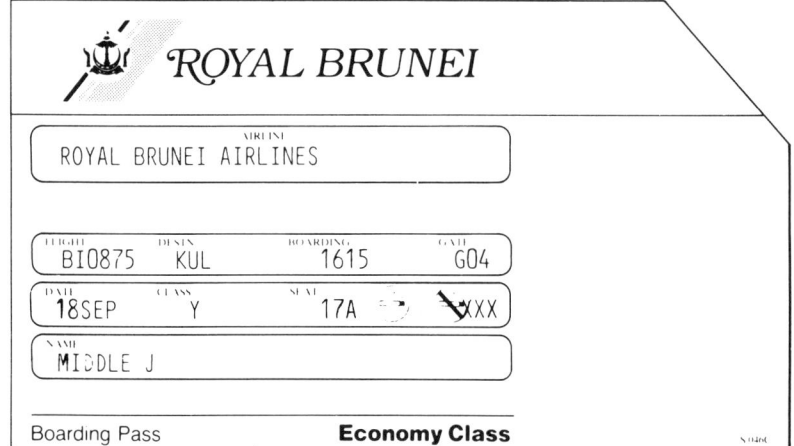

Lufthansa

Einsteigekarte / Boarding Pass

Flug/Flight, Datum/Date: LH 032 /04DEC
Abruf/Boarding Gate: A05
Zeit/Time: 12.10
Dest.: LON
Status:
Y 005
Sitzplatz/Seat: 005

L = Links/Left, Nichtraucher/Nonsmoker
R = Rechts/Right, Raucher/Smoker

ROYAL BRUNEI

AIRLINE: ROYAL BRUNEI AIRLINES
FLIGHT: BI0875
DESTN: KUL
BOARDING: 1615
GATE: G04
DATE: 18SEP
CLASS: Y
SEAT: 17A
XXX
NAME: MIDDLE J

Boarding Pass — Economy Class

Seats are numbered in rows from the nose of the aircraft (the front) to the tail and lettered from the right to the left as you look back from the flight deck.

On flights that do not have seats allocated and on which smoking is allowed, you should indicate to passengers which area is for smokers and which area is for non-smokers.* Flights for which seat allocation is not made are generally single-class flights.

---

* Note that on some flights smoking is totally forbidden.

Boarding

1 Why is it not necessary on most flights to allocate seat numbers to passengers as they board the aircraft?

2 How can you tell where a passenger should sit?

3 Where, approximately, would the following seats be? (Assume a Boeing 747)

row 17   row 34
seat A   seat H

Listening 4

Listen to the examples of cabin attendants' exchanges with passengers A to G and match them with the following situations.

1. A passenger is sitting in the wrong seat. ☐
2. A passenger wants to change her seat to be next to the window, but it is occupied. ☐
3. A passenger sits in a seat allocated to a CA. ☐
4. A passenger lights a cigarette in a no-smoking area or during preparation for take-off. ☐
5. A passenger is sitting in the first class cabin but has an economy ticket. ☐
6. A passenger cannot find his seat. ☐
7. Two passengers are arguing over the same seat. ☐

Language practice

Note that most seat allocation problems involve the CA requesting to see passengers' boarding cards. There are several ways of doing this:

May I see Would you mind showing me Can I ask you to show me I'm sorry, but I need to see I'm sorry, but I must ask you to show me	your boarding card

(Avoid using 'I'm afraid ...', meaning 'I'm sorry ...'. Although both are used in English, a passenger with poor English might misunderstand 'I'm afraid'.)

1 *Rewrite the following sentences so that you say the same thing in a more polite way. Use the words in brackets.*

(a) Put out your cigarette! (Would ... mind ... ?)
(b) Can't you find your seat? (Are you ... trouble ... finding ... ?)
(c) You have made a mistake! You are in someone else's seat! (... think ... may be ... wrong seat)
(d) Please change seats with this passenger. (Would ... mind ... ?)

2 *You will notice how some of the verbs need a gerund to complete the sentence and others need an infinitive:*

Gerund

keep	_____ ing
have trouble	_____ ing
mind	_____ ing
avoid	_____ ing
stop (someone)	_____ ing

Infinitive

remember	to _____
don't forget	to _____
ask (someone)	to _____
need	to _____

Use these constructions to advise passengers politely about:

- where to put their hand luggage
- controlling their children's movements during take-off
- rearranging their luggage in the overhead compartment
- reading the flight safety leaflet
- moving down the aisle as they find their seats
- not obstructing the emergency exits

3 *In pairs, practise your own dialogues between CAs and passengers with seating problems. Use the language from exercises 1 and 2.*

Boarding 25

STOWAGE OF BAGGAGE

What are these cabin attendants doing? Why?

Listening 5

Listen to the exchanges between cabin attendants and passengers. Fill in the table below.

	What is the problem/situation?
1.	
2.	
3.	
4.	
5.	

Language practice

Using the tables below, practise your own dialogues between cabin attendants and passengers.

Passenger:

I'm sorry but I'm having trouble with Where can I put Could you look after	my this	coat briefcase hold-all bag duty-free bags	?

CA:

May I Could I ask you to Do you think you could	stow place put	your	overcoat briefcase shoulder-bag hold-all bag	in the overhead comparment? in the wardrobe compartment? beneath the seat?

WELCOME ANNOUNCEMENT

What do you think the cabin attendant is saying here?

Boarding 27

Listening 6 🔊

Once all the passengers have taken their seats and all cabin baggage has been stowed, a general welcome announcement should be made. Very often it is recorded. Sometimes a cabin attendant makes the announcement.

Listen to this model announcement and complete the table below.

Flight No.	
To	
	90 minutes
Altitude	
Captain	
Requests	1.
	2.
	3.
	4.
	Smoking in the toilets

Language practice

Practise making similar announcements with these alternatives.

1. Morning / Lee / Singapore Airlines / SIA 62 / Bangkok / Bangkok / two hours and ten minutes / 32 000.
2. Morning / Al-Qahtani / Saudia / SDI 874 / Dhahran / Dhahran / 55 minutes / 28 000.
3. Evening / Cebrian / Iberia / IBE 727 / Malaga / Malaga / three hours / 31 000.
4. Evening / Ebe / All Nippon Airways / ANA 914 / Tokyo / Tokyo / six and a half hours / 29 000.
5. Afternoon / Oppicelli / Alitalia / AZA 577 / Sao Paulo / Sao Paulo / three hours and 25 minutes / 27 000.

SAFETY ANNOUNCEMENTS AND DEMONSTRATIONS

Oxygen masks

▲ CA reading corresponding announcement into microphone.

● 'required' CA giving cabin demonstration

✱ (if appropriate) additional CA giving cabin demonstration.

Cabin crew positions for demonstrating emergency equipment

Listening 7

Before any flight in an airliner, it is necessary for a demonstration of the use of oxygen masks to be given, together with an explanation. Although this is often done by video, cabin attendants should be capable of making the announcement.

Listen to this typical announcement, which you can read below at the same time.

Ladies and gentlemen.
Our cabin pressure is controlled for your comfort, but should it change at anytime during the flight, an oxygen mask will automatically fall from the unit above your seat. If this happens, please extinguish your cigarette immediately, pull down the mask and place it firmly over your mouth and nose. Secure the mask with the strap, as the cabin attendants are demonstrating. Continue to breathe normally, until you are advised that the oxygen masks are no longer required. A detailed safety instruction card may be found in the seat pocket in front of you.

Language practice

Practise giving this announcement yourselves. The pictures at the top of the next page may help you.

Boarding

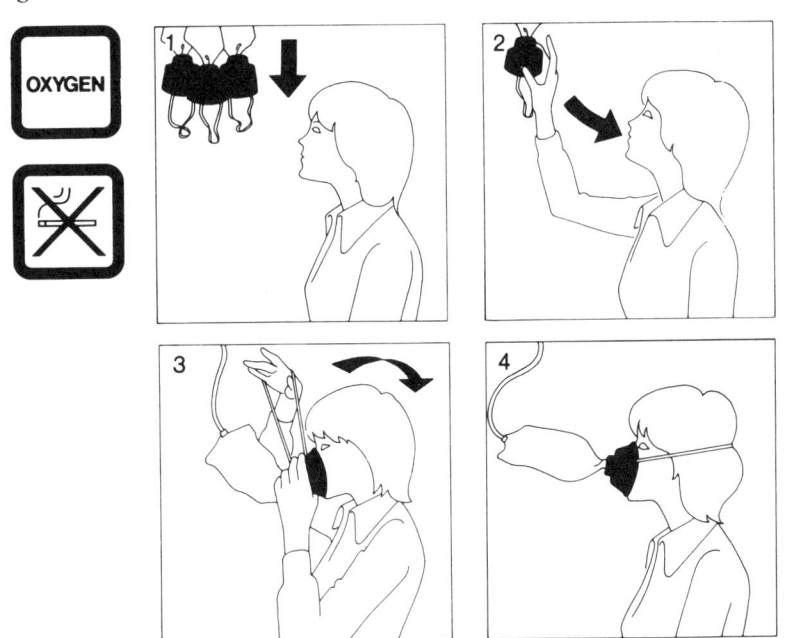

LIFE JACKETS

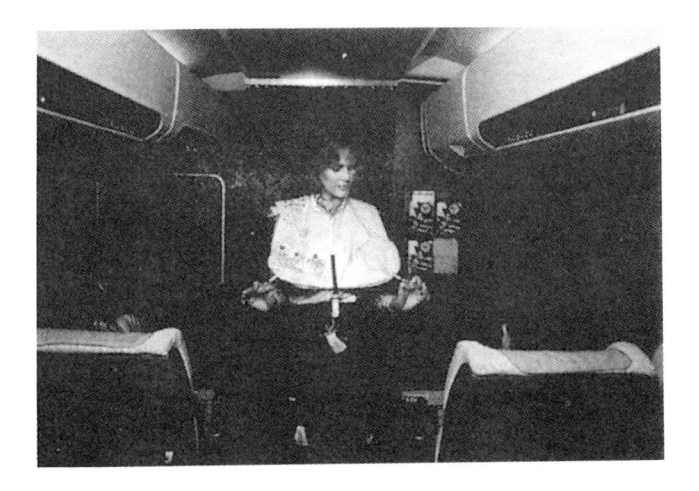

The CA in this picture is demonstrating the use of a life jacket, or life vest as it is also called. For flights over water, it is necessary to demonstrate the use of life vests. The need to do this is determined not only by the route of the flight, but also by the location of the airport.

Listening 8 🎧

Listen to this typical announcement, which you can read below at the same time.

Ladies and gentlemen.
As part of our flight today is over water, international regulations require that we demonstrate the use of the life jacket. Each passenger is provided with a life jacket which is located beneath your seat. Your cabin crew is now demonstrating how to use it.

Pull the life jacket over your head.
Fasten the jacket with the tapes around your waist as the crew are now demonstrating.
Do NOT, repeat NOT, inflate the jacket until you have left the aircraft.
The jacket is automatically inflated by pulling these tags, or, if necessary, by blowing into this tube.
A light is provided here, and a whistle for attracting attention.
Thank you for listening.

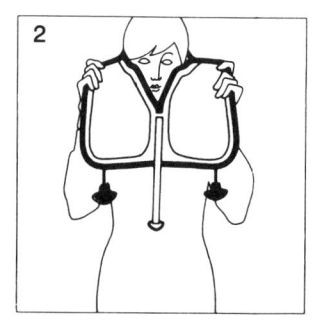

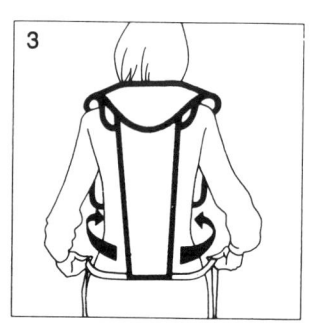

Language practice 1

Practise giving this announcement yourselves. The following pictures may help you.

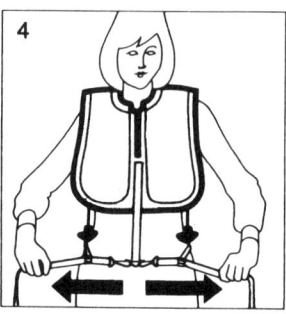

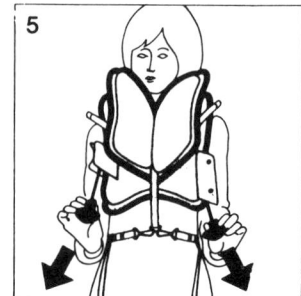

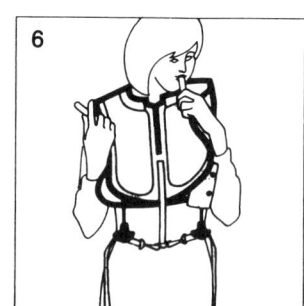

Boarding 31

Language practice 2

A passenger is concerned because he did not understand an announcement about seatbelts. Using the pictures as a basis for preparing your answer, how would you explain the use of the seatbelt? Avoid giving the worried passenger orders, but instead use these forms:

> First of all, you should ...
> Then you ...
> Next you ...
> After you've done that, ...

It is important to check that the passenger has understood:

> Is that clear?
> Does that make sense?

Also show him that he has understood:

> That's right.
> Good.

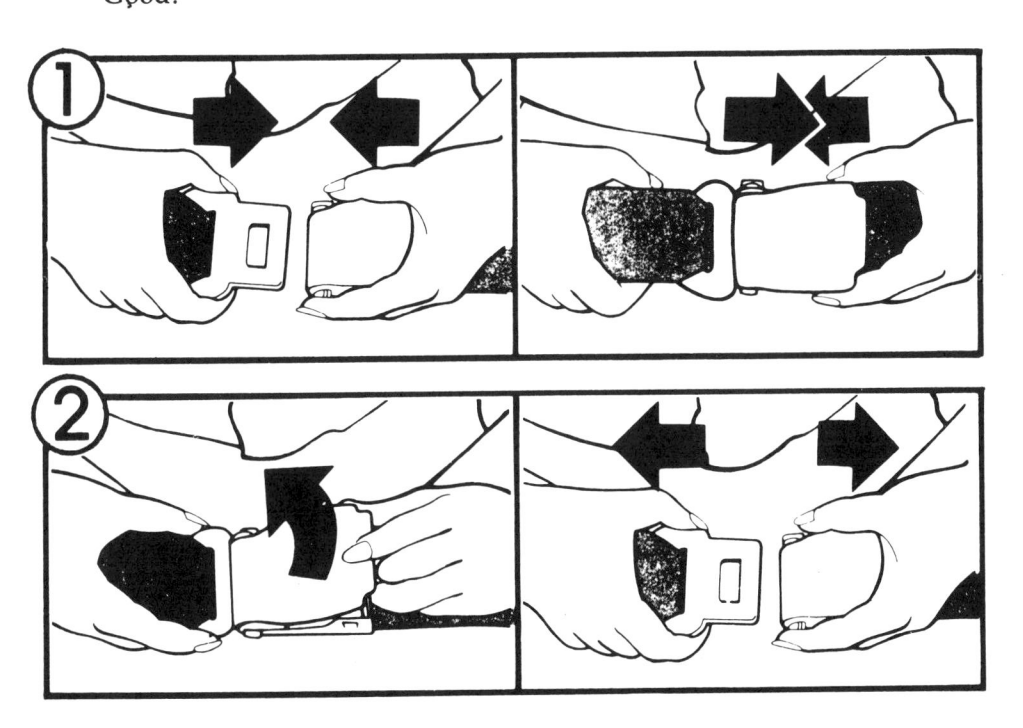

Use the following words as appropriate:

> tongue   flap   buckle

Useful words and phrases summary

briefing
on schedule
turbulence
VIP
CIP
UM
stowage
baggage
oxygen mask
life jacket/vest
weather conditions
delayed
diverted
fire extinguisher
first aid kit
boarding card
height

altitude
cabin pressure
strap
inflate
to brief (the crew)
Welcome on board ...
May I ...
Could I ...
Would you mind ...
Can I ask you to ...
Please extinguish your cigarette
Push your seatbacks into the upright position
Smoking in the toilets is forbidden
Keep your seatbelts fastened
On behalf of ... I wish you a pleasant flight
Breathe normally

> I hope this plane doesn't fly faster than sound — my friend and I have a lot to talk about!

UNIT 3

TAKE-OFF AND INITIAL FLIGHT

RAMP DUTIES

Reading

Read the text and do the exercise.

Once passengers are settled and the doors closed, the duties of CAs depend upon the time available before the airliner leaves the ramp (usually by pushing back from the airport terminal), taxies to the runway, lines up and takes off. The length of this time is predictable and planned but, if an airport is particularly busy with traffic taking off and landing, there may be a delay, or the captain may wish to hasten the departure.

Although this time is used for passenger services, the essential job of the cabin crew is to check that:

(a) there is no smoking;
(b) seatbelts are fastened;
(c) seats are in the fully upright position;
(d) tables are stowed;
(e) young children and babies sitting on an adult's lap are held firmly outside the seatbelt or, if available, within the supplementary seatbelt;
(f) all movable galley and catering equipment is secured as appropriate;
(g) internal doors and curtains between different parts of the cabin are secured open;
(h) overhead luggage compartments are closed.

Passenger services at this time vary from airline to airline and from class to class. They may include the provision of:

(a) boiled sweets to prevent ear problems;
(b) complimentary drinks;
(c) reading material;
(d) gifts which promote the airline;

(e) pillows, blankets, slippers;
(f) assistance for mothers with babies and/or young children;
(g) games and comics for children.

Place the following take-off procedures in the correct order. The first has been done for you.

Leave ramp	☐
Take off	☐
Line up	☐
Close doors	1
Taxi to runway	☐
Push back	☐

Listening 1

Listen to the summary of CA duties before take-off, and complete this checklist.

RAMP DUTIES FOR CA

Passengers
(1)
(2)
(3)

Babies
(1)

Cabin equipment
(1)
(2)
(3)
(4)

Language practice

1 *Practise making the following requests to passengers, using the words in brackets, so that the requests are more polite.*

Example: I'm sorry smoking is not allowed. (mind/put out/cigarette)
   Would you mind putting your cigarette out?

Take-off and Initial Flight

(a) Seatbelts must be fastened. (please/fasten)
(b) Your seat must be fully upright. (mind/put/seat upright?)
(c) Tables must be folded away for take-off. (may/ask/fold away/table?)
(d) You mustn't put your seatbelt around your baby. (would/like me/get/ supplementary seatbelt?)

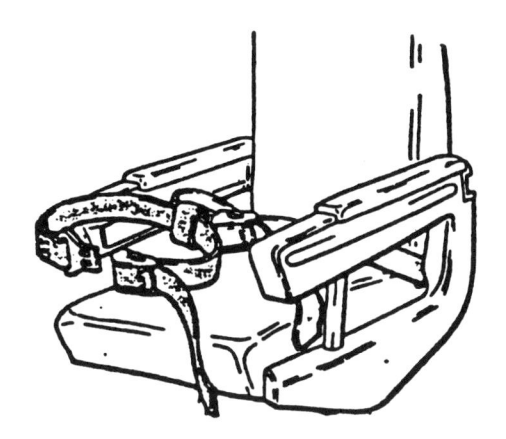

Use the checklist above to make more polite requests.

2 *Using the following models, ask passengers if they would like the items indicated.*

Would you care for	a sweet a drink	for your ears	sir	?
May I offer you	a newspaper a pen	with our compliments	madam	
Would you like	a pillow	for your comfort		

(a) a newspaper
(b) a sweet
(c) a pen
(d) a pillow
(e) a drink
(f) headphones
(g) a magazine
(h) a hot towel
(i) slippers
(j) games
(k) a blanket

TAKE-OFF PROCEDURES

Reading

Read the following text and answer the questions.

For take-off, CAs must also of course be seated with seatbelts secured. CAs must therefore listen carefully for the captain's announcement 'Ladies and gentlemen, we will be taking off very shortly'. This should be taken to mean 'CAs to take-off positions'. On a night flight, a member of the cabin crew should dim the cabin lighting at this point.

Take-off positions vary from aircraft type to aircraft type. On any particular airliner, positions depend on the number of CAs on board. The following example is given for illustration only.

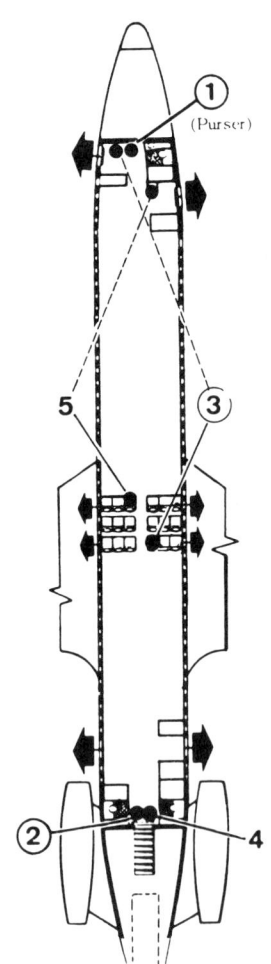

①②③ Full aircraft "required" CAs. (See. G. 112)

POSITION	AIRCRAFT	
	NOT FULL	FULL
①	LH/FWD Bench seat	
②	AFT Bench seat	
③	AFT Right overwing exit	LH/FWD Bench seat
4	AFT Bench seat	
5	FWD left overwing exit	FWD galley jump seat

Cabin crew positions for take-off and landing.
LH = left-hand; FWD = forward;
AFT = rear or behind.

Take-off and Initial Flight 37

The major take-off positions, such as position 1 in the diagram opposite, are known as 'stations'. The CA station contains the CA control panel, and is often located next to a galley, which is the area where food and drinks are prepared.

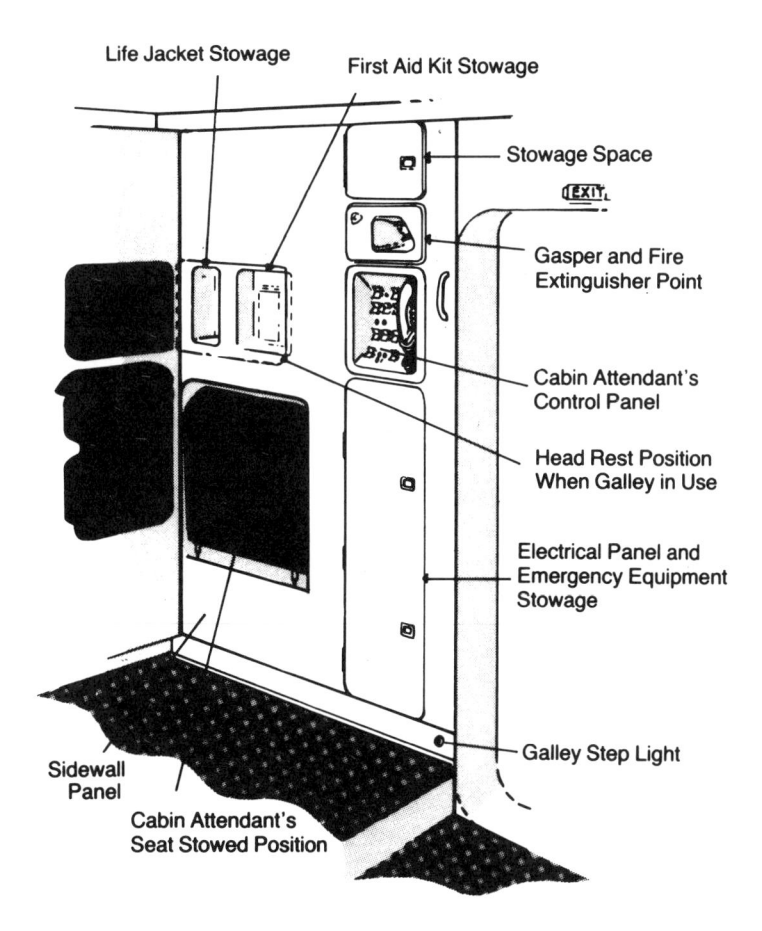

CAs remain seated with seatbelts fastened until the 'no smoking' sign is turned off by the captain. If a passenger starts to break one of the safety requirements, the CA who notices it should try to correct the situation with a spoken warning.

A general view of the requirement for CAs to remain seated with seatbelts fastened is given below.

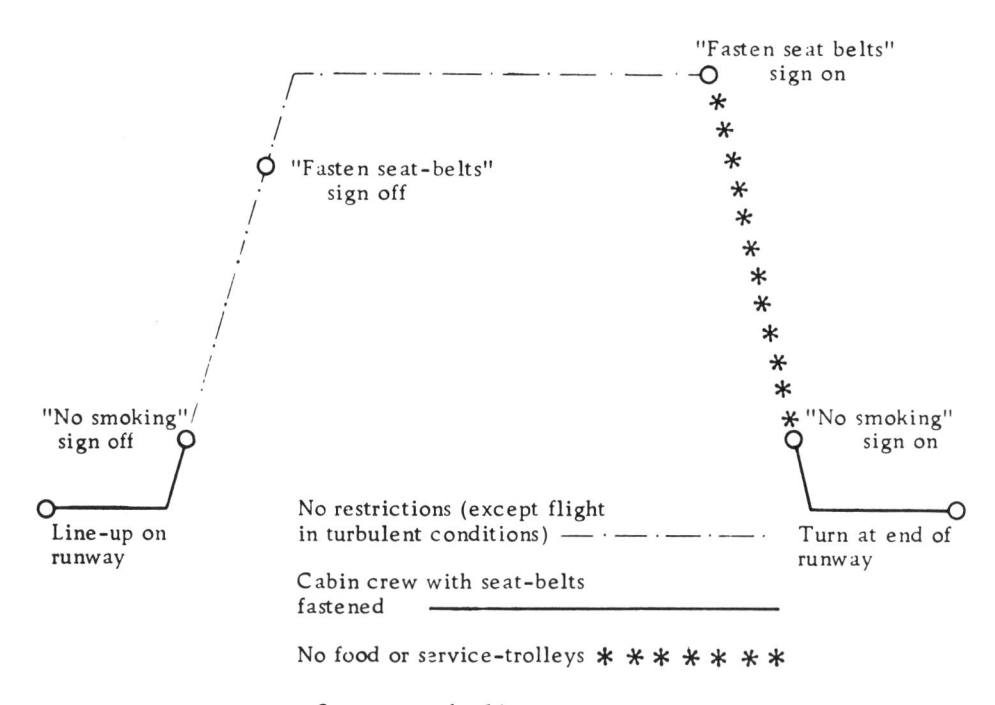

```
                                                     "Fasten seat belts"
              ┌─────────────────────────────○         sign on
              │                             *
              │                             *
              ○ "Fasten seat-belts"         *
              │  sign off                   *
              │                             *
              │                             *
              │                             *
              │                             *
              │                             *
              │                             *
              │                             *
"No smoking"  │                             * "No smoking"
 sign off  ○──┘                             ○─ sign on
 ○──────┘       No restrictions (except flight    └──────○
Line-up on      in turbulent conditions) ─·──·──·─  Turn at end of
runway                                               runway
                Cabin crew with seat-belts
                fastened               ─────────────

                No food or service-trolleys * * * * * *
```

Summary of cabin crew positions.

1 As a CA, how would you know when to sit down for take-off?
2 What are 'stations'?
3 Why do you think the CA stations are usually near a galley?
4 What sort of items would you expect to find on the CA control panel?
5 When can CAs leave their seats after take-off?

Useful words and phrases summary

take-off   Do you mind ...
ramp   Please ...
taxi   I'm sorry ...
galley   I'm sorry you'll have to ...
push back   Would you care for ...
line up   May I offer you ...
upright   Would you like ...
stow

UNIT 4
FOOD AND DRINK

MEALS

Reading

Read the text and do the exercise.

The type of service depends on the time of day, the class of passenger and the length of the flight leg. The main meals served are breakfast, lunch, dinner and snacks.

In general, first-class passengers receive a restaurant-type service, with a choice of food, and economy-class passengers receive a pre-set tray without variations or choice.

Breakfast

Breakfast can be a light meal consisting of a croissant or roll, with jam or marmalade, with fruit juice and tea or coffee. This is a 'continental breakfast'. A larger meal with perhaps a cereal and grilled bacon, sausage and eggs is known as an 'English' or 'cooked' breakfast.

Lunch/dinner

These more substantial meals are served at midday and in the evening respectively. They typically consist of:

> soup or hors d'oeuvres
> main course of meat or fish with a selection of vegetables
> dessert
> cheese and biscuits
> (fresh fruit)
> tea or coffee

This is an example of internationalised cuisine. Many carriers prefer to offer food of their own national cuisine.

Snacks

Snacks are small items of food served between main meals. They may vary from elaborate open sandwiches or fresh fruit and cheese to a simple packet of biscuits.

Food and Drink

Pre-set trays for economy-class passengers may be partially or completely pre-set, that is, prepared on the ground before flight. If the main course is cold, a salad for example, then all the CA has to do in terms of serving the meal is distribute the trays.

Pre-packed hot main courses are often provided, however, and have to be re-heated in the galley and added to the partially pre-set tray.

Trays should not be distributed silently, but with a pleasant remark:

    Here we are, sir.
    Lunch, madam?
    Would you care for a snack?
    I'm sorry, sir, but could you pass this tray to the passenger by the
      window.
    Excuse me, madam.

From the meals below find examples of:

    continental breakfast
    lunch
    dinner
    international cuisine
    a national dish
    a snack

- cous cous
- scone and butter with fruit preserves / tea
- fruit juice / croissant with jam
- fresh fruit and cheese
- lamb curry
- lasagne
- cake and coffee or tea
- boeuf en croute / selected vegetables / fruit salad and cream / cheese and biscuits
- a packet of salted nuts and a soft drink
- open sandwich
- chicken chasseur / rice and peas / chocolate cake

Food and Drink

Listening 1 🎧

Listen to the examples of passengers' comments about in-flight meals. Complete the information in the table below.

Passenger	Problem or request
1	
2	
3	
4	
5	

Language practice

1 *Match the passengers' comments on the left with suitable expressions by CAs on the right.*

Passenger
(a) No beef for me.
(b) Do you have a vegetarian dish?
(c) What's in the main dish?
(d) I'm not hungry.
(e) Can I have just a snack?
(f) How is the salmon cooked?
(g) Can I have the chicken instead?

CA
(i) It's poached.
(ii) How about chicken?
(iii) Yes, I think so. Did you order one?
(iv) Yes, what exactly would you like?
(v) It's beef with a mushroom sauce.
(vi) I'm sorry, there's no more chicken.
(vii) Would you like something else instead?

2 *Practise distributing meals to economy passengers in pairs. Student A (the passenger) should attempt a variety of questions or comments. Student B (the CA) should use a selection of the following expressions:*

- Here we are, sir
- Would you like some dinner madam?
- Could you pass this tray to the passenger by the window?
- Lunch, madam?
- Would you care for a snack?
- Excuse me, madam

Listening 2

Using the following menus (A and B), respond to the passenger questions and comments on the tape. Remember that not all passengers using English speak it fluently or correctly.

Menu A	Menu B
Fresh asparagus spears with butter	Ardennes pâté
	Prawn cocktail
Cream of tomato soup californienne	
Chicken kiev	Roast sirloin of beef
Lamb biryani	Smoked haddock mornay
Raspberry sorbet	Coupes St Jaques
Black Forest gateau	Fruits of the forest soufflé

Working with a partner, prepare a menu for a meal you might expect to find served on your national carrier. Then practise dialogues of your own between the CA and the passenger.

Food and Drink

SILVER SERVICE

Silver Service is the name of the formal waiter/waitress service offered to first-class passenger. How is the food in the picture above different from that on pp. 39–40?

In what other ways is the first-class service usually different?

Listening 3

Listen to the examples of CAs addressing passengers in the first-class cabin and practise repeating the phrases.

Language practice

1 *Practise making questions or statements to first-class passengers, as politely as possible, from the following cues:*

1. Offer soup or hors d'oeuvres.
2. Offer a choice of lamb biryani or chicken kiev.
3. Offer a choice of roast sirloin of beef or smoked haddock mornay.
4. Check that the passenger enjoyed the meal.
5. Offer tea or coffee.
6. Check why the passenger hasn't eaten.

COMPLAINTS

Language practice

1 *Match the passengers' complaints and queries about their food (1—7) with the appropriate response from the CA (A—G)*

1. 'You haven't given me any potatoes.'

2. 'I'm sorry, but this pork is absolutely stone cold.'

3. 'Haven't you got any Brazilian coffee?'

4. 'Are you sure this lobster is fresh?'

5. A passenger points at her beef curry and says, 'This cow or pig or sheep?'

6. 'Please. What is this?'

7. 'This food is absolutely appalling.'

A. 'I'm sorry, madam, but you'll appreciate we are restricted in what we can carry on board. The Arabica and Tanzania bean is an excellent blend.'

B. 'I'm very sorry, sir. I'll get the purser to come and have a word with you.'

C. 'It's apple strudel, madam, an Austrian dish of apple wrapped in pastry.'

D. 'It's beef, madam. From a cow.'

E. 'Yes, sir. I can assure you that it is.'

F. 'I do apologise, sir. I'll see to it immediately.'

G. 'I'm terribly sorry, sir. I'll bring you some immediately.'

Food and Drink

2 *Complaints and queries will arise with both kinds of service. The table below gives passenger prompts. The second column gives extra information, if appropriate and available, to help you form your answer. What do you say in each situation?*

The passenger says:	You, the CA, know that:
1. 'This food is cold.'	
2. 'Oh God. I've spilled my drink.'	
3. 'Can I have another main course?'	There is one available.
4. 'Can I have another main course?'	There isn't one available.
5. 'This chicken stinks of garlic.'	Chicken kiev, which is what the menu says clearly, always contains garlic.
6. 'This fish is off!'	No-one else has complained.
7. 'This fish is off!'	Several other passengers have complained.
8. 'There aren't any knives or forks.'	They are wrapped up in a serviette on the passengers' tray.
9. 'There aren't any knives or forks.'	There aren't any knives or forks on the tray.
10. 'That was delicious. Can I have the recipe, do you think?'	
11. (Passenger has not touched the food, but says nothing).	
12. 'That was absolutely disgusting!'	

DRINKS SERVICE

In all classes, soft drinks are complimentary. In first class, alcoholic drinks are also complimentary. In all classes, the same sort of language is used:

What would you like to drink, sir?
Can I get you anthing to drink, madam?
Would you care for a drink, sir?

Listening 4

The specific language of alcoholic drinks is outside the scope of this book, but you need to be familiar with a basic range of drinks. Listen to the passengers' drinks orders and match them with the descriptions.

1. Vodka and tomato juice ____
2. Champagne and orange juice ____
3. Whisky and ice ____
4. Vodka and orange juice ____
5. White rum and cola ____
6. Tonic water ____
7. Vodka and tonic water ____
8. Whisky ____
9. Beer with lemonade ____
10. Lemonade, squash, water etc. ____
11. Irish whiskey with coffee ____
12. Rye whiskey ____

After a meal, tea and coffee are usually served.

Food and Drink

Language practice

Bar Tariff		LIQUEURS	£1.00
Wines ¼ bottle	£1.00	Cointreau, Drambuie, Tia Maria, Coffee Liqueur (except Domestic Services)	
Red and white (except Highlands & Islands Services)			
*Champagne (also chargeable on Intercontinental flights in Economy) (not on Domestic Services)	£2.00	VERMOUTH	50p
		Dry or Sweet (except Highlands & Islands Services)	
SPIRITS Miniature	£1.00	SHERRY (except Highlands & Islands Services)	50p
American, Canadian, Irish Whiskey & Campari (except Domestic Services) Scotch Whisky, Gin, Vodka, Cognac & Rum		BEER/LAGER Can	50p
		ALL SOFT DRINKS are Complimentary	

1 *Practise this dialogue, in pairs, between a CA and a passenger. Use the bar tariff chart.*

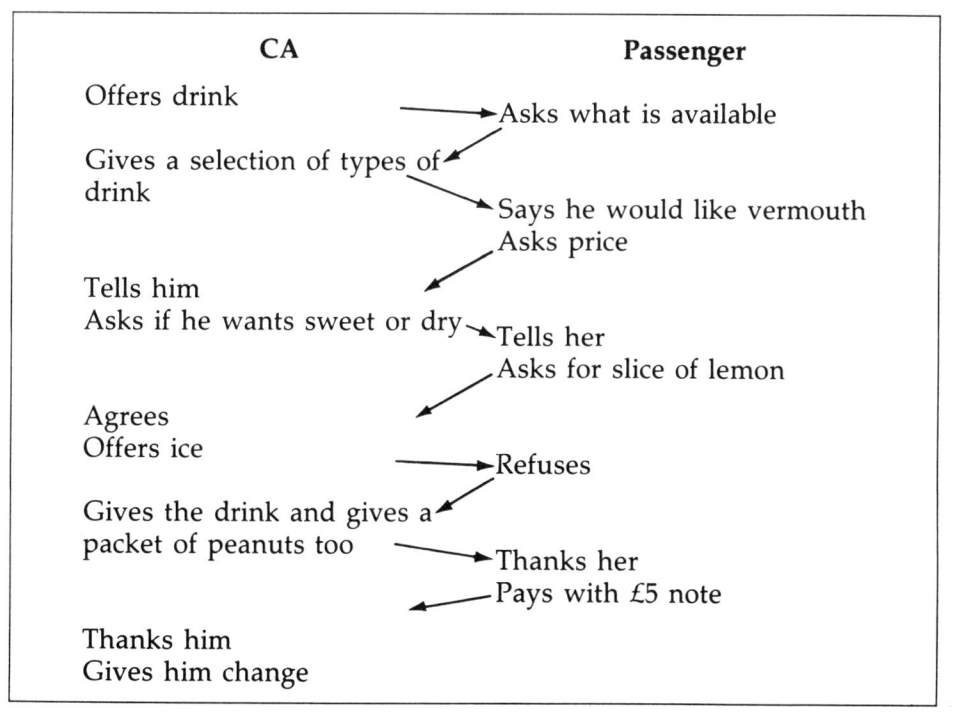

CA	Passenger
Offers drink →	Asks what is available
Gives a selection of types of drink ←	
	→ Says he would like vermouth
	Asks price
Tells him	
Asks if he wants sweet or dry →	Tells her
	Asks for slice of lemon
Agrees	
Offers ice →	Refuses
Gives the drink and gives a packet of peanuts too ←	
	→ Thanks her
	← Pays with £5 note
Thanks him	
Gives him change	

Now practise with other drinks.

2 *Using the bar tariff practise dialogues between CAs and passengers, in pairs. The following passenger requests may help.*

Do you have any wines?
I fancy a liqueur.
Vermouth, please.
A beer, please.
What have you got in the way of spirits?
How much will that be?

3 *Look at this table of flying times and answer the questions which follow.*

	Athens	Cairo	Dublin	Düsseldorf	Lima	Los Angeles	Madrid	Muscat	Rome	Singapore
Athens	—	2	$4\frac{1}{2}$	4	$15\frac{1}{2}$	13	3	6	2	11
Cairo	2	—	6	$4\frac{1}{2}$	$16\frac{1}{2}$	$14\frac{1}{2}$	$5\frac{1}{2}$	4	3	10
Dublin	$4\frac{1}{2}$	6	—	2	$14\frac{1}{2}$	$11\frac{1}{2}$	$2\frac{1}{2}$	10	3	16
Düsseldorf	4	$4\frac{1}{2}$	2	—	25	$12\frac{1}{2}$	$2\frac{1}{2}$	9	3	15
Lima	$15\frac{1}{2}$	$16\frac{1}{2}$	$14\frac{1}{2}$	15	—	9	13	22	14	26
Los Angeles	13	$14\frac{1}{2}$	$11\frac{1}{2}$	$12\frac{1}{2}$	9	—	$11\frac{1}{2}$	$20\frac{1}{2}$	$12\frac{1}{2}$	17
Madrid	3	$5\frac{1}{2}$	$2\frac{1}{2}$	$2\frac{1}{2}$	13	$11\frac{1}{2}$	—	7	2	16
Muscat	6	4	10	9	22	$20\frac{1}{2}$	7	—	$7\frac{1}{2}$	6
Rome	2	3	3	3	14	$12\frac{1}{2}$	2	$7\frac{1}{2}$	—	$13\frac{1}{2}$
Singapore	11	10	16	15	26	17	16	6	$13\frac{1}{2}$	—

What meal service would you expect to find on these flight legs?

(a) Singapore to Muscat departing at 21.30.

_____

(b) Dublin to Düsseldorf departing at 08.55.

_____

(c) Athens to Madrid departing at 17.50.

_____

Food and Drink

(d) Cairo to Rome departing at 11.05.

(e) Lima to Los Angeles departing at 12.30.

4 *To help blind passengers, the position of items on a tray should be given by reference to a clock face. For example 'At one o'clock' 'At six o'clock'.*

Explain the position of the following items on the tray above.

    Container with cheese, biscuits, butter and jam in it
    Dish of Spanish omelette with sausages and mushrooms
    Cutlery wrapped in a serviette
    Fruit salad
    Glass with container of cream in it
    Orange juice
    Yogurt

Begin:

At one o'clock there is a small glass of orange juice in a cup.

EQUIPMENT

The standard of galley depends upon the size of the airliner. In aircraft such as the Boeing 747 a number of large galleys are provided.

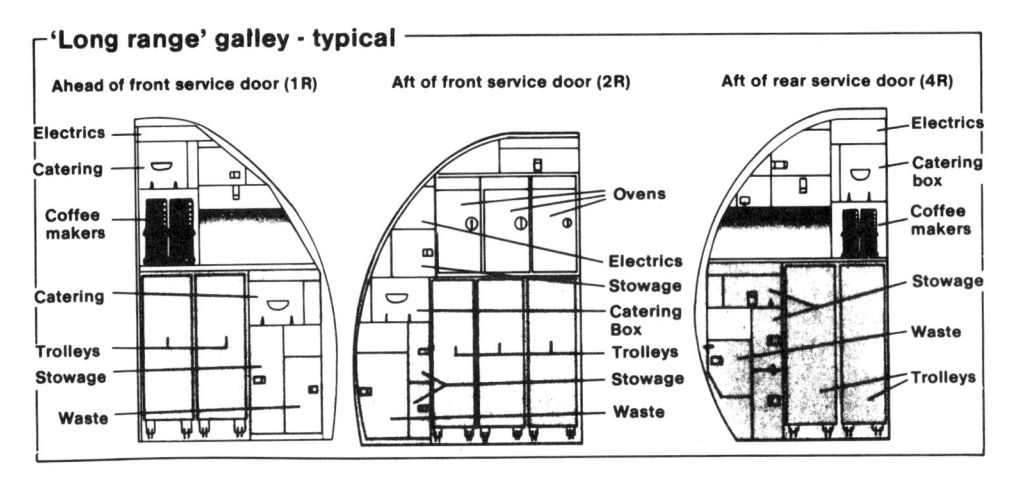

'Long range' galley - typical

Ahead of front service door (1R): Electrics, Catering, Coffee makers, Catering, Trolleys, Stowage, Waste

Aft of front service door (2R): Ovens, Electrics, Stowage, Catering Box, Trolleys, Stowage, Waste

Aft of rear service door (4R): Electrics, Catering box, Coffee makers, Stowage, Waste, Trolleys

These are typical galleys fitted in a British Aerospace 146.

Listening 5

On the tape, a purser briefs a new CA on the Shorts 360 galley. Write in the names of the units on the diagram:

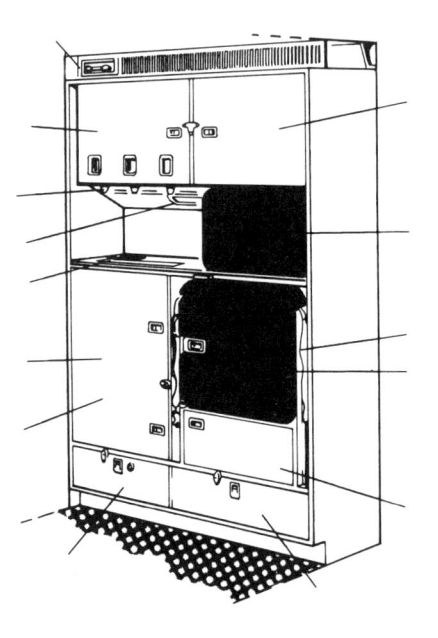

Food and Drink

Language practice

Look at the diagram of the meal trolley and see if you can explain how it is used. Mention facilities for hot and cold food, and for securing the trolley.

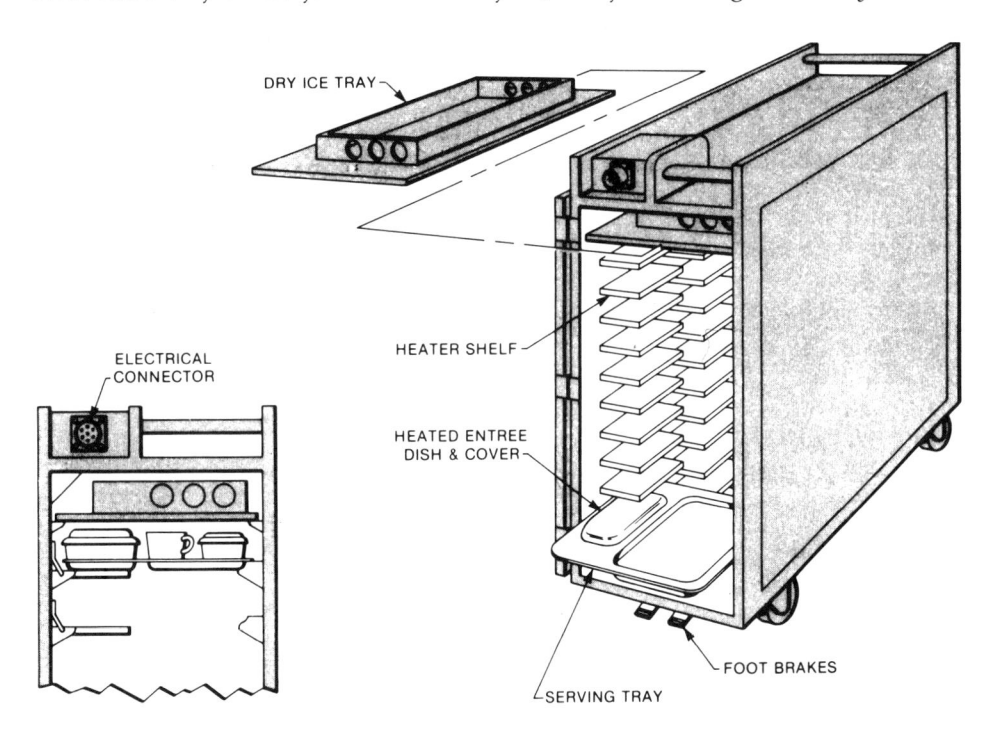

Diagram labels: DRY ICE TRAY, ELECTRICAL CONNECTOR, HEATER SHELF, HEATED ENTREE DISH & COVER, SERVING TRAY, FOOT BRAKES

Useful words and phrases summary

leg (i.e. part of journey)
snack
pre-set tray
pre-packed hot meals
re-heated
storage
I'll get you another
I'll see to it immediately
That will be (£1.00)
Would you care for ...?
Would you like some ...?
May I take ...?
Have you finished ...?
We can offer you ...?

continental breakfast
English breakfast or cooked breakfast
entrée
hors d'oeuvre
main course
a selection of vegetables
lamb
beef
chicken
pork
fish
rice
potatoes
sausages

UNIT 5

IN-FLIGHT ENTERTAINMENT

MOVIES/FILMS

Reading

During longer flights, a movie (American and airline standard English), or film (British English), may be shown.

An announcement is necessary in order to:

(a) Give brief information about the film.
(b) Inform passengers about headsets and any charge for them on international flights.
(c) Allow passengers to change seats for a better view.

The announcement describes the type of film it is.

Match the following types of film with the correct description.

(i) drama (a) a film to make viewers laugh
(ii) drama documentary (b) a serious film telling a real-life story
(iii) thriller (c) a serious film
(iv) comedy (d) a crime or spy story

Can you think of any other kinds of film? Give an example of the four kinds above:

drama _____

drama documentary _____

thriller _____

comedy _____

Because children are often on board, airlines try to choose films which are suitable for family viewing. If this is not the case, the above categories should be prefixed with the word 'adult' e.g. adult drama.

Listening 1

A member of the crew usually makes an announcement about the films being shown. Listen to the following typical announcement and then try it yourself, repeating if necessary:

Ladies and gentlemen.
We shall shortly begin our feature film which we hope you will enjoy watching. Today's film is entitled *Return to Errol*, a drama starring Lindsay Horne, David Tough and Jack Herd. Headsets are obtainable from the cabin crew, and the English sound track of *Return to Errol* is on channel 1 for the first class cabin and channel 2 for economy class.
Music is available on the other channels and details are given in the *In-Flight Magazine*, which may be found in the pocket of the seat in front of you. International regulations require us to make a charge for the hire of the headset. If you would like to change your seat, please inform a member of the cabin crew.
Thank you.

Language practice

Practise making in-flight movie announcements using either the information given in Table A or information you have prepared for Table B (next page).

Table A

Film	Type	Stars
Burnished Shades of Delight	drama	Scott Robertson and Laura McNae
Surely that was one of your other husbands!	adult drama	David Perry and Jill Ryder
The Bedhampton Crossing	thriller	Hugh Papworth
Pooch	comedy	Frank Nugent and Robert Critchley
Auntie Herma	drama documentary	Anna Scott and John Griffith
Was that a Yes or a No?	adult comedy	Victoria Alexander

Table B

Film	Type	Stars
1.		
2.		
3.		
4.		
5.		

Not all passengers will want to hire earphones.

The timing of each part of a CA's duties is important.

In-flight Entertainment

PASSENGER ARM-REST CONTROLS

Reading

Read the following text and do the exercise.

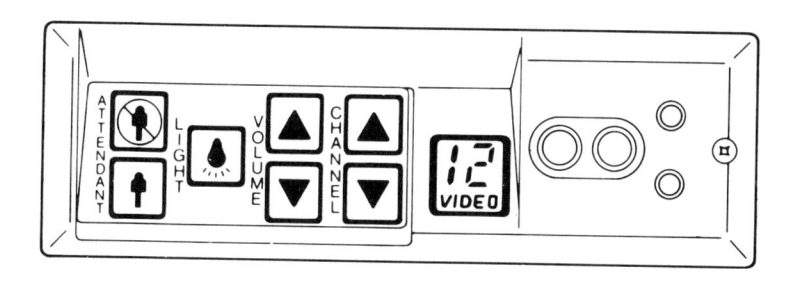

The simplest arm-rest contains only an ashtray and a release button for reclining the seat. High levels of in-flight entertainment, however, require passenger control units like the one illustrated above. The controls in this unit are, from left to right:

(a) attendant call buttons
(b) light switch
(c) volume controls for a headset
(d) channel selector buttons for the audio system
(e) channel indicator
(f) socket for a pneumatic headset
(g) socket for an electrical headset

Attendant call buttons and light switch are more often located in the passenger service unit (see next section). In some cases, the headset socket(s) are separately located on the front face of the arm-rest.

In pairs practise dialogues between a CA and a passenger who wants the arm-rest controls explained. Use these expressions:

Passenger: What is this for?

How do I ⎰ make the music louder?
         ⎱ get the film soundtrack?
         ⎱ switch on my reading light?

CA:

This ⎰ socket
     ⎱ button   is for ... ing ...
     ⎱ control

PASSENGER SERVICE UNITS

Language practice

1 *Above each group of seats is a passenger service unit often having three functions. It may be necessary to show the inexperienced passenger what it is used for. Study the diagram below and practise dialogues between a CA and a passenger, in pairs, using the models given.*

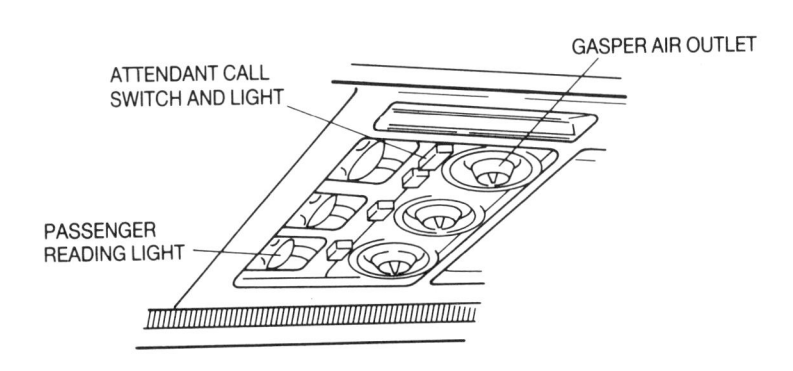

Models

Passenger: It's very hot and stuffy in here.
I can't see to read my book.
How can I call you in future?

CA: If you adjust this nozzle, you can control the direction and amount of air conditioning.
This button controls your individual reading light.
If you press this button, it will light up at the end of the cabin and one of us will come to your assistance.

2 *Practise passenger/CA dialogues based on the following situations:*

(a) A passenger wants to read while the cabin lights are turned down.
(b) A passenger feels in need of air.
(c) A passenger cannot hear anything through the headset.
(d) A passenger can hear music through the headset but she wants to hear the film soundtrack.

PASSENGERS' READING MATERIAL

On longer flights, in first class, newspapers and magazines are distributed.

The initial question by a CA might be:

>Can I offer you something to read, sir?
>Would you care for a newspaper, madam?

A positive reaction, spoken in English, would prompt the CA to say, for example:

>I have *The Times*/the *Daily Telegraph*.
>We can offer you the *Economist*/the *Financial Times*.

Language practice

Practise these exchanges with a partner:

1. **CA:** Can I offer you something to read, sir?
   Passenger: What newspapers do you have?
   CA: We have *The Times*, the *Telegraph* and the *Financial Times*.
   Passenger: I'll have *The Times*, please.

2. **CA:** Would you care for a newspaper, madam?
   Passenger: Do you have the *Daily Telegraph*?
   CA: No, I'm sorry, but I do have *The Times*.
   Passenger: Then I suppose that'll have to do.

3. **Passenger:** Do you have anything to read? You know, newspapers or magazines.

	CA:	Which would you prefer, sir? We have both.
	Passenger:	A couple of magazines would be fine.
	CA:	There you are, sir.
	Passenger:	Thanks very much.
4.	CA:	Would you like a magazine, madam?
	Passenger:	Do you have any in *French*?
	CA:	No, I'm sorry. They are all in *English*.
	Passenger:	Never mind. Thank you anyway.

Useful words and phrases summary

drama
documentary
thriller
comedy
headset
earphones
volume
channel
socket
switch off/on

turn off/on/down/up
plug in
pull out
Pressing this button …
This button operates …
This socket is for …
If you press this button …
This button controls …
You can adjust …

UNIT 6

DUTY-FREE SALES

PRELIMINARY ANNOUNCEMENTS

Listening 1

Listen to the announcement and complete the missing items.

Ladies and gentlemen.
We shall ... commence the ... of duty-free goods. ... details of our selection of cigarettes, ... perfumes and other ... are given in the *In-Flight Magazine* which you will find in the seat ... in front of you.
On today's flight we can ... French francs, pounds Sterling and dollars. Travellers cheques and major credit cards are also accepted.
May we ... that our rates of exchange are ... rates which are not necessarily the current bank rates.
Thank you.

Try practising this accouncement yourself, repeating if necessary.

Listening 2

Listen to the announcement on the tape and complete the table below, naming what is available or acceptable.

Eau de toilette _____

Perfume _____

Aftershave _____

Alcohol _____

Tobacco _____

Currency _____

Plastic (Credit/charge card) _____

Listening 3 🎧

Listen to the exchanges and complete the table below.

Dialogue	Summary of situation
1.	_____
2.	_____
3.	_____
4.	_____
5.	_____
6.	_____

Study the following models:

I am very sorry but   we have sold out
                                  we have none left
                                  we do not carry that brand
                                  we do not have any small bottles
                                  we only have the eau de toilette
                                  we cannot accept that currency

How about the aftershave?
The Aramis is very popular.

Language practice

1 *Look at the situations below and give appropriate responses. Use the words in brackets, where given.*

(a) A passenger asks for a brand of cigars you do not carry.
(b) A passenger asks for a brand of whisky you have sold out of.
(c) A passenger asks you to recommend her an eau de toilette (Gucci spray/very popular).
(d) A passenger asks for Rothmans cigarettes. You do not have any. (Dunhill or Peter Stuyvesant).

2 *Think of questions from the CA that would produce the following responses from passengers:*

(a) I don't want anything too expensive.
(b) A box of twenty-five will do.
(c) Could I see both brands, please?
(d) That will do.
(e) About fifteen to twenty pounds.

Duty-free Sales

(f) I'll take the Johnny Walker.
(g) Not this one; the other one please.
(h) Chanel No. 5, please.
(i) I think this one is best.
(j) I'd rather have the larger one, please.

3 *Use this table of duty-free items to practise dialogues between CAs and passengers.*

Produce	Quantity	Normal price	In-flight price
Perfumes and toiletries			
Miss Dior atomiser, eau de toilette	60 ml	£21.00	£14.00
L'Air du Temps, Nina Ricci eau de toilette	60 ml	£18.50	£13.50
Channel No. 5 perfume	50 ml	£25.00	£21.00
Aramis aftershave	60 ml	£11.00	£9.50
Gifts			
Ladies' pure silk scarves (Yves St Laurent)	Size: 90cm × 90cm	£62.00	£39.50
Colibri coliseum II Cigarette lighter		£28.00	£20.00
Cigarettes			
Benson and Hedges Special Filter	200	£15.00	£7.50
Drinks			
Beefeater gin	$\frac{1}{2}$ litre	—	£3.00
Johnnie Walker whisky	$\frac{1}{2}$ litre	—	£5.00

Please note these prices are given for training purposes only.

DUTY-FREE ALLOWANCES

Reading

Passengers may want to know about duty-free allowances in the destination country. (This information should be checked at the briefing.)

Use the information below, which is only given for training purposes, to determine whether the statements beneath are true or false.

		Cigarettes	Cigars	Tobacco	Wine	Spirits	Perfume
Gibraltar		200	or 50	or 250 gm	2 ltr	1 ltr	50 gm
Hong Kong	V	200	or 50	or 250 gm	1 ltr	or 1 ltr	60 ml
	R	100	or 25	or 125 gm	1 ltr	Nil	60 ml
Hungary		250	or 50	or 250 gm	2 ltr	1 ltr	fpu
India		200	or 50	or 250 gm	1 btl	or 1 btl	fpu
Iran		200	or 750 gm	or 750 gm	Nil	Nil	¼ ltr
Iraq		200	or 50	or 250 gm	1 ltr	or 1 ltr	½ ltr
Ivory Coast		200	or 25	or 25 gm	1 btl	1 btl	
Jamaica		200	or 50	or ½ lb	2 ltr	1 ltr	nl
Japan	V	400	or 100	or 500 gm	3 btl	or 3 btl	2 oz
	R	200	or 50	or 250 gm	3 btl	or 3 btl	2 oz
Jordan	V	200	or 50	or 200 gm	2 btl	or 1 btl	fpu
	R	200	or 50	or 200 gm	1 btl	or 1 btl	fpu
Kenya		200	or 50	or ½ lb	1 btl	or 1 btl	1 pint
Korea	R	200	25	100 gm	1.5 ltr	or 1.5 ltr	2 oz
	V	400	50	200 gm	1.5 ltr	or 1.5 ltr	2 oz
Kuwait		200	50	500 gm	Nil	Nil	fpu
Liberia		200	or 25	or 250 gm	1 ltr	1 ltr	fpu
Malawi		200	or 250 gm	or 250 gm	1 ltr	1 ltr	Nil
Malaysia		200	or 50	or 225 gm	1 ltr	or 1 ltr	nl
Malta		200	or 225 gm	or 225 gm	1 btl	1 btl	fpu

V visitors   fpu for personal use
R residents   nl   no limit

(a) Visitors to Kuwait are allowed two bottles of wine. True/False
(b) Visitors to India are allowed 50 cigars, as long as they have no cigarettes. True/False
(c) Visitors to Jamaica are allowed as much perfume as they wish. True/False
(d) Visitors to Kuwait may take as much perfume as they wish for presents. True/False
(e) Visitors to Jordan are only allowed one bottle of wine. True/False
(f) Visitors to Liberia are allowed 25 cigars. True/False
(g) Visitors to Hong Hong are not allowed any spirits. True/False
(h) Visitors to Kenya are allowed half a pound of tobacco. True/False
(i) Visitors to Iraq are allowed half a litre of perfume. True/False
(j) Visitors to Malaysia may take as much perfume as they wish, provided it is for personal use. True/False

Duty-free Sales

> I've just run out of cigars — keep an eye out for a box of Havanas.

Useful words and phrases summary

duty-free
spirits
in-flight magazine
bar tariff
rate of exchange
brand
a selection of ...
I'm very sorry (indeed) ...

We have sold out of ...
You will appreciate that ...
... is very popular
... make(s) a very acceptable present
Our pleasure
It's no trouble at all
We have none left
We do not carry that brand

UNIT 7

GENERAL PASSENGER QUERIES AND PROBLEMS

TECHNICAL

Reading

Passengers will ask questions covering a very wide range of technical matters to do with the aircraft's performance.

Typical questions and suggested responses are given in the table below, but they have been mixed up. Match the correct response to each question.

Passenger's question	CA response
(On take off/landing) What was that loud bang?	It's a rather technical subject, sir/madam, but basically the air moving at speed over our wings creates a lifting force that is equal to our weight.
The wings seem to be bending!	All the important pieces of aircraft systems are at least duplicated, sir/madam.
I think one of the engines is on fire!	It was the wheels locking up/down, sir/madam. Don't worry. It's perfectly normal.
I've never understood. How exactly are we keeping in the air?	Relax, sir/madam! All the cabin crew are highly trained. And, in any case, I'm sure nothing is going to go wrong. So just sit back in your seat and enjoy the flight.

General Passenger Queries and Problems 67

How on earth does the pilot know which way to steer?	Jet engines work with a flame coming from their exhaust, sir/madam. There's absolutely nothing unusual about that.
How can it be safe to fly through all this cloud?	Yes, sir/madam. They are designed to be flexible. In fact, if they weren't they wouldn't be safe!
What if something breaks down?	Don't worry, sir/madam. Our Captain is using radar and the latest radio navigation systems.
What would we do if the worst came to the worst?	Well, sir/madam, he has very sophisticated electronic equipment up on the flight deck, and he uses this to navigate towards radio beacons, which are located on the ground.

Listening 1

Listen to the passengers' questions and complete the chart below.

Passenger	Situation/problem
1	
2	
3	
4	
5	
6	

Language practice

In pairs, practise exchanges between passengers and CAs like those above. Students playing the role of the CA should use these expressions to help them:

> I shouldn't worry about that.
> It's quite normal for the *engine* to *make that noise*.
> There's no need to worry.
> Don't worry.

DESTINATION INFORMATION

Passengers on international flights often want information about the destination if they have never visited it before. They hope that you, the CA, will be able to share your personal experience. If it is your first visit to the particular country, do not be tempted to give information unless you are very sure of your general knowledge. Instead, say:

I'm sorry sir/madam. I have only just transferred to this particular route. I'll ask one of my colleagues to come and help you.

Listening 2

Listen to the exchanges between passengers and CAs and complete the missing words:

1. Do you think I'll need a _____ when we land?

   I don't think so, madam. It's still quite warm in Barcelona at this _____ of year.

2. Will I be all right in this dress or do you think I _____ put a cardigan on?

   Well, you _____ know. Perhaps it would be safer to wear _____ cardigan.

3. Is it easy to _____ a hotel _____ in Kuwait?

   You _____ have any _____ at this time of year.

4. How am I going to get into the city?

   You can take a taxi, or the information desk in the _____ building will be _____ to advise you about public transport.

General Passenger Queries and Problems 69

5. I have a _____ flight to San Antonio. Any idea what I _____ do?

6. Any idea what the _____ is like in Rome?

Yes sir. When we _____ Dallas, you _____ at the transfer desk.

I'm not sure but the captain will _____ just before we land.

Language practice

Study these ways of giving advice:

I would recommend taking a taxi.
If I were you, I should wear a coat.
I think you should make a reservation.
You shouldn't have any trouble at this time of year.
It would be better to ask at the information desk.

Now practise giving advice to passengers in the following situations. Use the words in brackets.

1. A passenger doesn't have any local currency. (change money/airport)
2. The city centre is a long way from the airport. (take/airport bus)
3. A passenger doesn't have a hotel reservation. (make a reservation/airport)
4. A passenger has a connecting flight. (go/Air France desk/airport)

TIME CHANGES

Listening 3

Listen to the exchanges about time differences and complete the information. The first one has been done for you.

1. A: What is the local time in Cairo now?
   B: They are 2 hours ahead, so it's 3.20, sir.
2. A: What time is in in ... ?
   B: One hour ... so it's ... sir.
3. A: What do I have to do to ... my watch to ... time?
   B: ... ... 5 hours, madam.
4. A: Do I need to ... my ... ?
   B: Yes, sir. Put it ... ... for Rome.
5. A: I've ... ... completely. What time and what day is it?
   B: It's ... 24th ... and ... in the ...
   A: Well, I've got the right ... on my watch, but it's ... 5.15 a.m.

Language practice

Note the following ways of expressing time difference:

+	−
2 hours ahead	1 hour behind
forward	backward
Put your watch forward	Put your watch backward
Wind your watch forward	Wind your watch backward

Now practise dialogues between passengers and CAs about time differences.

Twenty-four-hour clock

Change these times to the 24-hour clock:

1. Half past three in the morning   *03·30*
2. Twenty to six a.m.   _____
3. Quarter to ten in the evening   _____
4. Ten past four a.m.   _____
5. Twenty-five to seven p.m.   _____
6. Five to twelve at night   _____
7. Quarter past twelve a.m.   _____
8. Twenty past one p.m.   _____
9. Twenty-five to nine a.m.   _____
10. Ten to two p.m.   _____

NURSING MOTHERS

Reading

An airliner is normally equipped with items to assist a nursing mother. A CA should therefore be familiar with all the items which a nursing mother might request. Can you identify these items in the picture?

feeding bottle
teats
powdered baby food
sterilising tablets
baby talcum powder

(disposable) nappies
 (Am.E. = diapers)
nappy pins
bottled/canned baby food
mixing jug

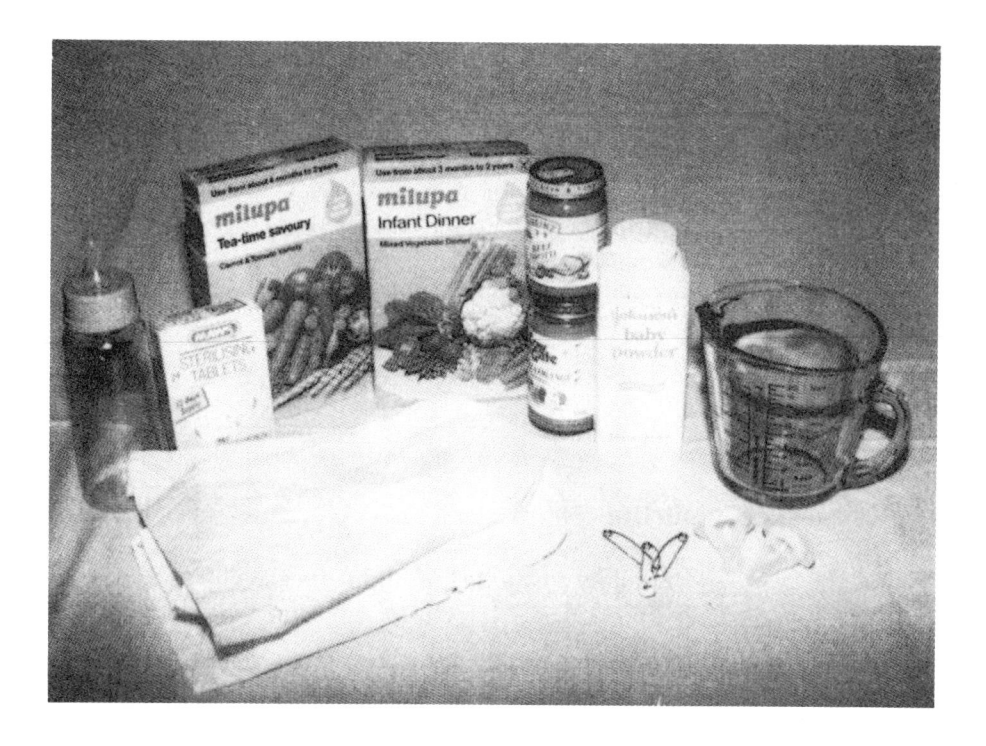

Large airliners carry a cot (British English), or bassinet (American English), that can be offered to a nursing mother.

Listening 4 🔊

Listen to the questions from nursing parents and complete the information.

Parent	What does s/he want?	What would you say/do?
1.		
2.		
3.		
4.		
5.		

Now match the following model replies to the five questions:

(a) I think so, sir. I'll just go and get some for you.
(b) We have gripe water on board. What do you think the trouble is?
(c) Yes. If you'd like to come with me.
(d) Of course. Do you need an extra blanket?
(e) Certainly. I won't be a minute.

MISCELLANEOUS

(A) Request to visit the flight deck

Whether the captain will allow visits to the flight deck will depend upon:

(a) airline policy;
(b) the nature of the particular flight, and thus the captain's work load;
(c) who is making the request, in the case of a CIP or a VIP.

(B) Use by passengers of portable electronic equipment

The use of electronic equipment by passengers may interfere with the radio navigational equipment on board the airliner. The particular items prohibited vary from airliner to airliner. CAs should be watchful for the following:

General Passenger Queries and Problems

Personal stereo (Walkman)

Electronic game

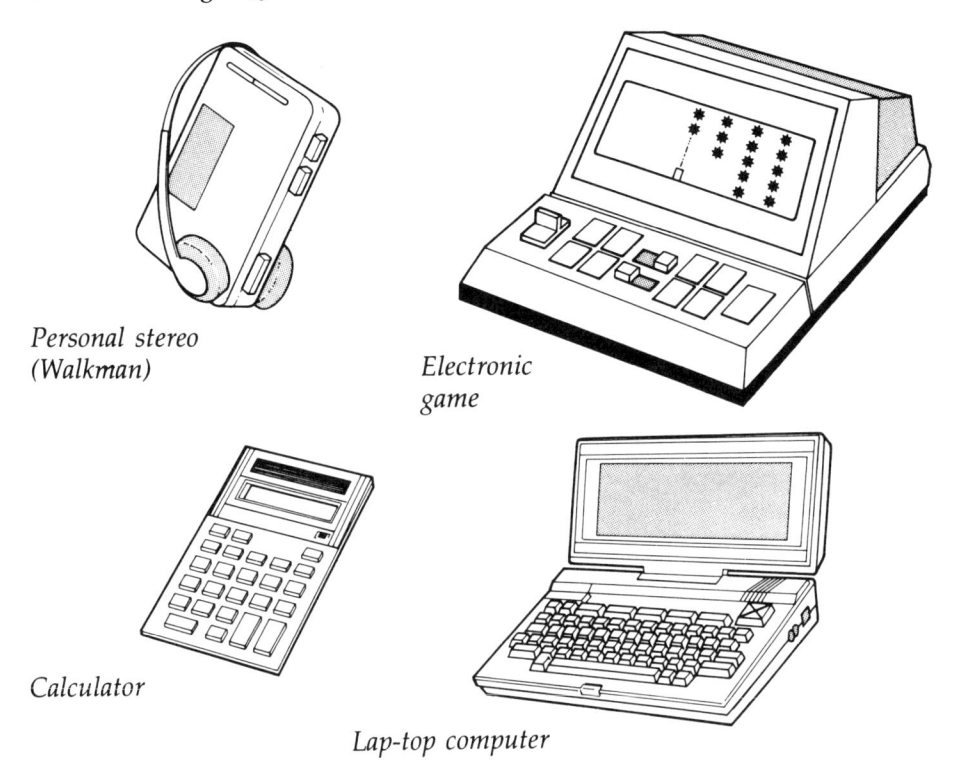

Calculator

Lap-top computer

Passengers using prohibited equipment must be told to stop.

(C) The passenger in the toilet

If a passenger spends an excessive amount of time in the toilet, he or she may be in distress.

A passenger in such a situation may feel too embarrassed to speak to a CA of the opposite sex, and you should offer to bring another CA.

If all attempts produce silence, the purser must be informed.

Note. A wide range of words may be used by passengers to mean 'toilet'. Some of the commonest are:

Word	Comment	
the loo	Slang British English.	Do not use yourself.
the blue room	American English.	Do not use yourself.
the john	Slang American English.	Do not use yourself.

(D) Reporting faults

Often you will report faults to an engineer of your own airline who speaks the same language. Sometimes, however, especially at destinations which your airline does not serve very regularly, the engineer will have a different mother tongue and you will have to report faults in English. Practise reporting faults in English using the illustration of the toilet and using the following models.

The *waste container* isn't working properly.
There's a fault with the *waste container*.
The *waste container* needs checking.
Could you check the *waste container* please?
The *waste container* isn't serviceable.

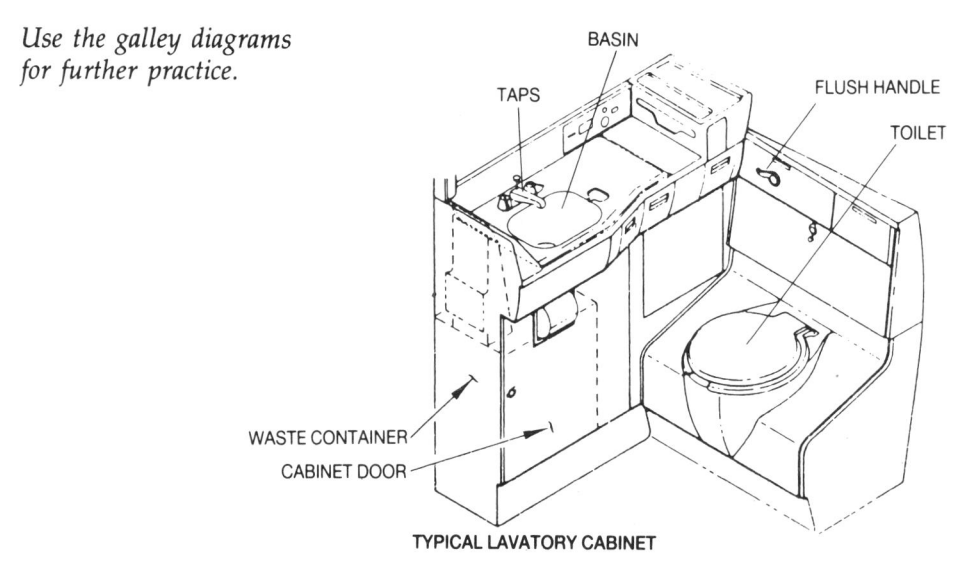

Use the galley diagrams for further practice.

TYPICAL LAVATORY CABINET

(Labels: BASIN, TAPS, FLUSH HANDLE, TOILET, WASTE CONTAINER, CABINET DOOR)

Listening 5

First read the situations described below. On the tape you will hear CAs speaking to passengers. Match the spoken words with the situation.

1. A passenger asks if he can visit the flight deck, and you expect the captain will say 'yes'. ☐
2. A passenger asks if she can visit the flight deck. You know from experience that the captain will probably not allow this. ☐
3. You see a passenger using a personal stereo, which is prohibited on the particular aircraft. ☐
4. A passenger refuses to stop using a lap-computer. ☐
5. A passenger has been in the toilet for a long period of time. ☐

General Passenger Queries and Problems

PASSENGERS' COMPLAINTS

Listening 6

Listen to the passengers' complaints and identify the problems.

Problem

1. _____
2. _____
3. _____
4. _____
5. _____
6. _____
7. _____
8. _____
9. _____
10. _____

Language practice

1 *Sometimes passengers have good reason to complain. At other times they are just troublesome. Your correct assessment of the situation is very important and your response should reflect this. Match the responses below with the complaints you heard.*

(a) I am terribly sorry. It should have been heated. Would you like another?
(b) I am sorry about this. I'll see if I can find a spare no-smoking seat.
(c) I'm sorry you think so. What exactly is the trouble?
(d) Oh dear. I don't know how that happened. I'll get you one right away.
(e) If you'd like to show me where, I'll have a word with the gentlemen.
(f) I'll come and see. What exactly is he doing that bothers you?
(g) Sorry about that. Which particular goods did you want?
(h) Yes I know. I've had a word with the mother. There's not a lot else we can do.
(i) I'll have a word with them.
(j) Really? I'll get someone to investigate immediately, sir.

2 *In pairs, practise making and responding to complaints. Decide in each case whether the CA's response is an apology, an explanation, a suggestion to improve things or a polite reprimand. Make use of the following expressions:*

I am sorry.
I'll see to it immediately.
I'll get you another.
I'll get *someone* to *investigate*.
I do apologise. It should have been *cleaned*.
What exactly is the problem?
I'll have a word with *the passenger concerned*.
I'm sorry I must ask you to *stop smoking*.
I'm sorry I'll have to speak to *the captain* about this.
I'm sorry but you are not allowed to *smoke here*.

DEALING WITH PROBLEMS AND QUERIES

Language practice

Match the passengers' problems and queries (1–7) with the appropriate response from the CA (A–G).

1. You haven't got any nappies on board, have you? He's got through rather more than I'd planned!
2. I've noticed a couple of passengers visiting the flight deck. Do you think I could?
3. Do you have any newspapers in Albanian?
4. I see you stopped that man using his calculator. I really need to use mine to prepare a report. Would it be all right?
5. And what are you doing later tonight, sexy?
6. I'm absolutely disgusted with the standard of service on this flight.
7. Do these jumbos have a cot on board by any chance?

A. I'll ask the purser to come and speak with you madam.
B. Yes indeed, madam. I'll bring you one straightaway.
C. Certainly, madam. I'll just get you some disposable ones.
D. I expect so, madam, but I'll have to check with the captain first.
E. Excuse me, sir. The purser wants to speak with me.
F. I'm sorry, we don't sir. Would you like one in English?
G. I'm very sorry, madam, but it's a matter of safety. They interfere with the aircraft's electronic systems.

General Passenger Queries and Problems

Useful words and phrases summary

nursing mother
personal stereo
electronic game
calculator
lap-top computer
to book a hotel
connecting flight
transit lounge
transfer desk
(one hour) ahead/forward
(one hour) behind/backward
nappy/diaper
sterlising tablets
gripe water

There's no need to worry
Don't worry
It's perfectly normal
Relax
We are expecting ...
There is a slight possibility ...
I'll check with ...
I'll have to check with ...
It's a matter of safety
I shouldn't worry about that if I were you
I'll see if I can find ...
Sorry. It should have been ...
I'll have a word with ...

UNIT 8

EMERGENCY PROCEDURES

CABIN DEPRESSURISATION

Reading

A sudden drop in cabin pressure is immediately noticed because of the sudden drop in temperature which accompanies it. As a result a fog forms in the cabin.

The immediate action of the captain is to put the aircraft into a steep dive down to an altitude which does not require the use of oxygen masks. He will also switch on both the 'fasten seat belt' and 'no smoking' signs. In more modern airliners, a pre-recorded announcement will automatically operate.

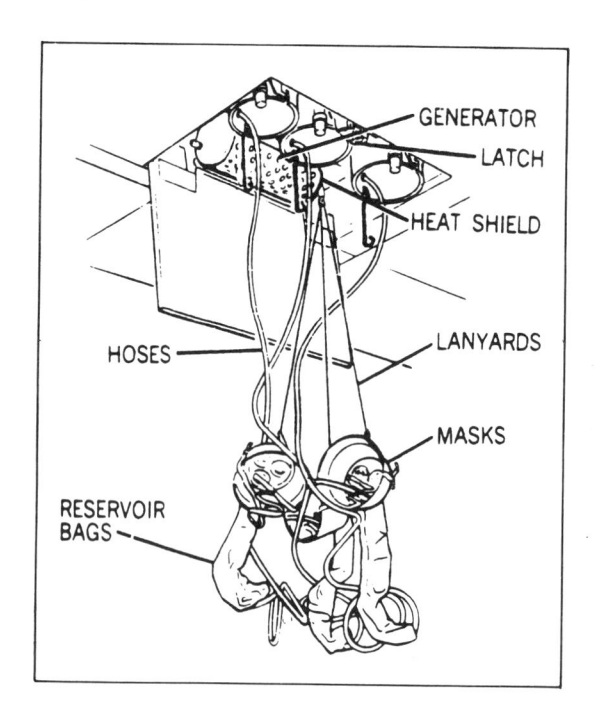

Emergency Procedures

The immediate responsibility of the cabin crew is to put on oxygen masks. This means the nearest available one. As soon as possible they should use the independent oxygen masks provided for CA use, although it may not be possible to reach one for several minutes, because of *g* forces, the aircraft's attitude etc.

Then, an announcement must be made, if it has not been made by the captain or co-pilot, or automatic recording, even though it may conflict with the general CA requirement to sit down and strap oneself in.

Listening 1

Listen to the emergency announcement and follow it with the text below.

Ladies and gentlemen.
Due to a loss of cabin pressure, we are making a rapid controlled descent for a few minutes to a safer altitude.
Please extinguish all cigarettes immediately. During this period, please use your oxygen mask. Pull it down, place it over your nose and mouth and breathe normally. Adjust the strap to secure the mask. Parents should adjust their own masks first, then assist their children. Please breathe through the masks until you are advised to remove them.
Thank you.

As soon as it is possible to move about, that is, when the descent has flattened out, all CAs should put on portable oxygen masks and assist any passenger having difficulty.

Language practice

Cover the announcement above and then match these pairs correctly. Then put them in a suitable order.

Please extinguish
During this period,
Please breathe through your masks
Adjust the strap
Parents should adjust their own masks first,
Pull it down,
Due to the loss of cabin pressure

please use your oxygen mask.
to secure the mask.
then assist their children.
place it over your nose and mouth, and breathe normally.
we are making a rapid controlled descent for a few minutes.
until you are advised to remove them.
all cigarettes immediately.

FORCED LANDING

Reading

It is to be hoped that you will never experience a forced landing. It is, fortunately, a very rare occurrence. Training in, and continued familiarisation with, such emergency procedures are essential. It is important to remember that most people on board survive most forced landings. The first few minutes following a forced landing are the most dangerous. Certainly, swift evacuation of the cabin will result in considerably more lives being saved than if the correct procedures are not carried out effectively.

The time available for a crew to prepare for a forced landing will vary from incident to incident. Precise evacuation procedures will vary from airliner to airliner. In every case, however, it is the captain who declares the emergency and orders the application of the emergency drill. The following is a generalised procedure and in dangerous situations there is not always time to do everything. National regulations may require different procedures.

The captain calls the senior cabin crew member (e.g. the purser in a small airliner) to the flight deck. The captain briefs him and gives the time he considers available. The purser returns to the cabin, securing the door to the flight deck in the open position.

The purser assembles the cabin crew, using the public address system if necessary. They will have been alerted by the unexpected switching on of both passenger signs by the captain.

The purser briefs the CAs and assigns duties. These will include the opening of all cabin separation curtains, stowage of all loose items and the preparation of emergency equipment. If the captain is preparing for a ditching, he may require that one CA is assigned to the flight deck to help put on life vests.

The purser then informs the passengers with an announcement.

Listening 2

Listen to the announcement and follow it below:

Ladies and gentlemen.
Please listen very carefully.
We have to make an emergency landing in approximately 15 minutes.
Your safety will depend on carrying out the following instructions carefully and calmly. Your crew have been especially trained for situations of this nature.
Please remain seated, extinguish all cigarettes, place your seat in the upright position and secure the table in front of you.
Refer to the card in the seat pocket in front of you for details of emergency landing procedures.
Listen for the next announcement shortly.

Emergency Procedures 81

Time may be too short for announcements in several languages. In the case of an international flight between countries with different mother tongues, English may be the appropriate language.

Language practice

1 *Reformulate the following sentences, keeping the same meaning, but using the words in brackets.*

(a) In about 15 minutes there will be a forced landing. (make/emergency/approximately)
(b) Do not leave your seats. (remain)
(c) Your seat must be upright and the table folded. (place/position/secure)
(d) You should read the emergency landing procedures on the card in the seat pocket. (refer/details/in front)

2 *Try to reproduce the announcements as closely as possible to the originals but using your own words if necessary.*

Reading

Read the text and do the exercises.

Emergency procedures normally require the use of selected passengers known as able-bodied passengers (ABPs) or pre-selected passengers (PSPs) to assist the CAs. The purser is responsible for selecting them and he will normally choose younger able-bodied men with an appropriate mother tongue. He briefs them on their duties, which are to assist CAs under order:

(a) to operate emergency exits when ordered;
(b) to stand near exits and assist other passengers to evacuate;
(c) if outside the aircraft, to hold the escape chute on the ground;
(d) if outside the aircraft, to assist passengers in clearing the area at the bottom of the chute;
(e) in the case of ditching, to throw out life rafts.

These pre-selected passengers are reseated next to the emergency exits. If necessary the other seats near to the emergency exits are emptied and children may be regrouped.

. CA POSITIONS

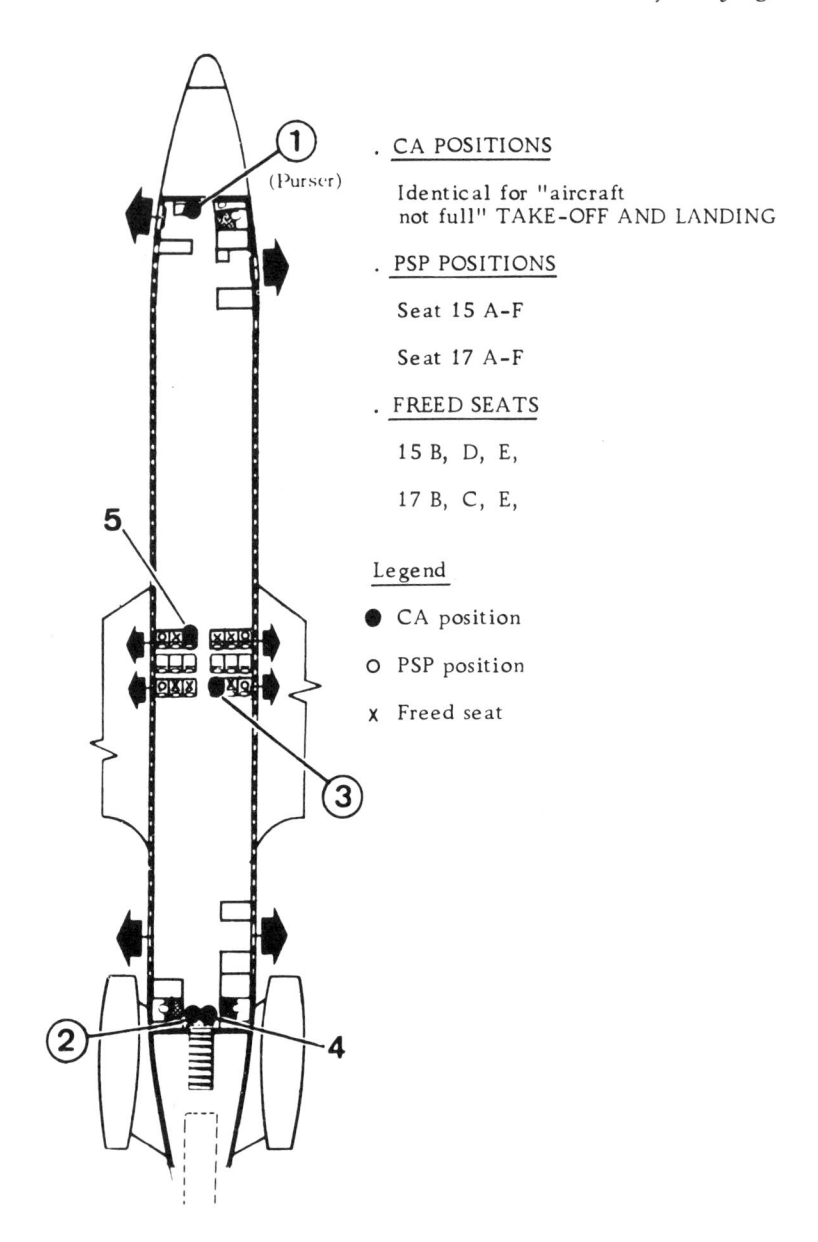

Identical for "aircraft
not full" TAKE-OFF AND LANDING

. PSP POSITIONS

Seat 15 A-F

Seat 17 A-F

. FREED SEATS

15 B, D, E,

17 B, C, E,

Legend

● CA position
○ PSP position
× Freed seat

1. In what way do passengers officially help with emergency procedures?
2. What sort of passengers are normally selected and who by?
3. Once these passengers have been told what to do, where do they go?

Emergency Procedures 83

Language practice

Reformulate these instructions to PSPs using the words in brackets:

(a) You want him to operate the emergency exits. (you must)
(b) He should position himself near the exits and help passengers leave the aircraft. (I want/stand/assist/evacuate)
(c) Outside the aircraft he should keep the end of the chute steady. (you must/hold/firm/ground)
(d) He must throw out the life rafts. (you have to)

EMERGENCY PROCEDURE ANNOUNCEMENTS

Listening 3

Listen to the emergency procedure announcements and repeat them, following the text in your book.

Note:
The instruction about life jackets is only made if a ditching is planned.

Please remove your shoes, glasses, dentures, pens and all sharp objects which might injure you.
Put on your life jacket but do not, repeat not, inflate it until you have left the aircraft.

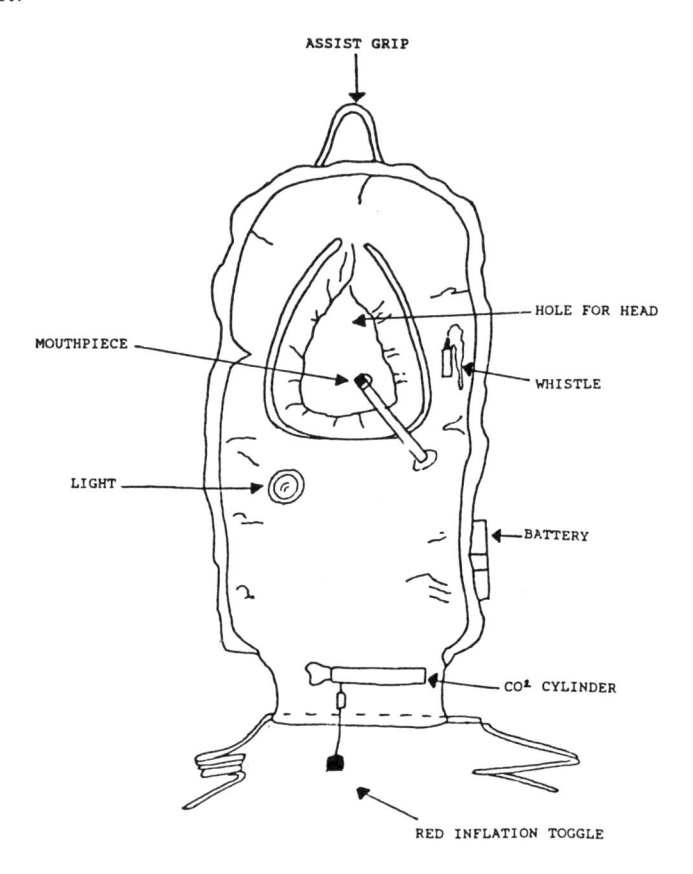

Fasten your seatbelt as tightly as possible after placing a cushion or a coat between the safety belt and your body.
When you hear the command 'brace for impact' or the 'fasten seatbelt' sign starts to flash, take the position we are now showing you.

Emergency Procedures 85

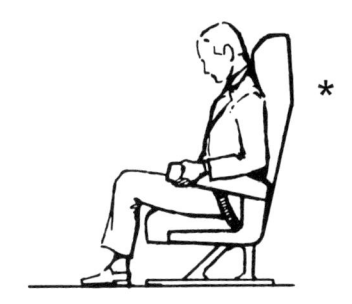

During the landing you will feel several sharp bumps.
Remain in the 'brace for impact' position with seatbelt fastened until the plane comes to a complete rest.
Wait for instructions before moving, and keep calm.

Language practice

You should know these announcements by heart in case you ever need to make them. However, you should be able to explain the procedures in your own words if necessary. Answer the following questions in the form of instructions to passengers, using the words in brackets to help you.

(a) What must I do about my shoes and glasses? (please/remove)
(b) What about the life jackets? (put/not inflate/before)
(c) Do I keep my seatbelt fastened? (fasten/cushion)
(d) What will it be like when we crash land? (feel/bumps)
(e) When can we leave the aircraft? (remain/position/halt)

Reading

Read the text and do the exercises.

CAs do not sit down and fasten their seatbelts until the captain's announcement:

'Touchdown in 30 seconds.'

The purser then announces:

'Brace for impact. Brace for impact.'

Some airlines use 'heads down' instead of 'brace for impact'.

---

* Whether huddled or upright position is appropriate depends on the pitch of the seating. The latter is used only with short-pitch seating.

CAs are trained to evacuate specific types of aircraft, and in each case in the post-impact situation, precise evacuation drills will depend on the suitability for use of each emergency exit. Here is a diagram of a typical evacuation system:

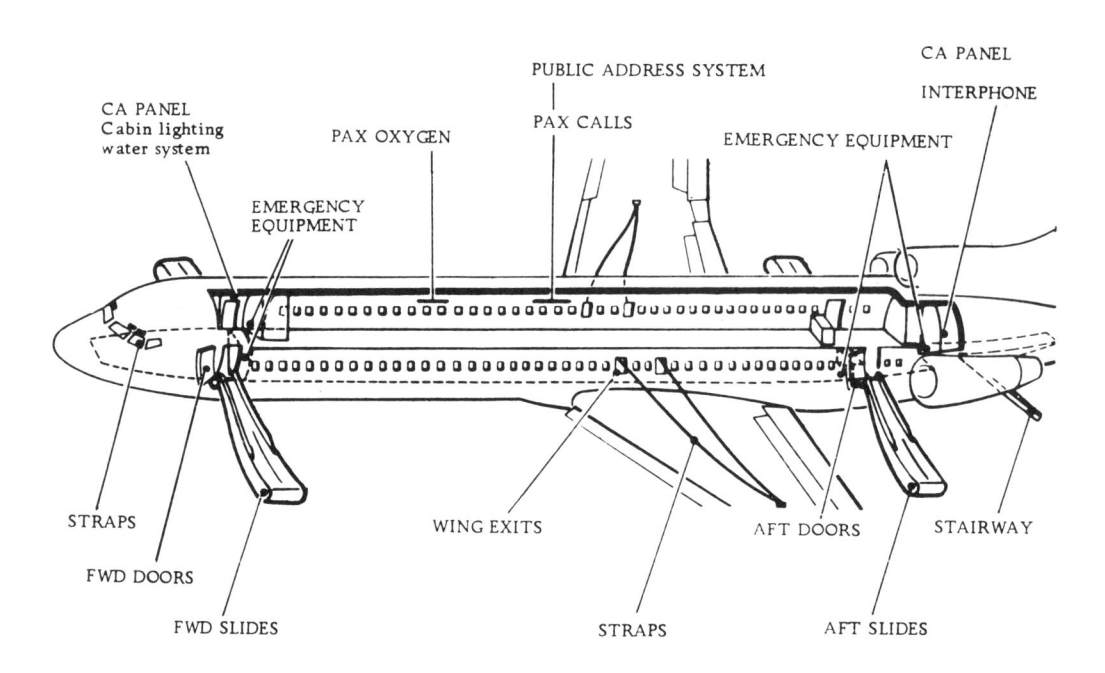

[Diagram: typical evacuation system showing CA PANEL (Cabin lighting, water system), EMERGENCY EQUIPMENT, PAX OXYGEN, PUBLIC ADDRESS SYSTEM, PAX CALLS, EMERGENCY EQUIPMENT, CA PANEL INTERPHONE, STRAPS, FWD DOORS, FWD SLIDES, WING EXITS, STRAPS, AFT DOORS, AFT SLIDES, STAIRWAY]

Orders should always be given in a positive form. For example, KEEP CALM should be used rather than the negative DON'T PANIC. Remember that to enable an orderly evacuation, the CAs must be seen and heard to be in control of the situation.

The following short, sharp orders are appropriate:

General

Unfasten your seat belt.
Evacuate now.
Leave your luggage.
Stop.

Non-use of emergency exit

Use opposite exit.
Use next exit.
That way.

Outside

Move away from the aircraft.
Swim towards that life raft.

Emergency Procedures 87

Use of emergency exit

Come.
This way.
Here.
Single file.
Double file.
Faster.
Slower.
Jump/Go (i.e. down the escape chute).
Move.

1 *Match the meanings below with the appropriate evacuation orders in the text above. Try to remember or guess the right orders before checking the text.*

(a) Passengers can get out of their seats.
(b) You tell passengers which direction to take.
(c) Tell passengers not to bother with collecting their bags.
(d) They are not moving quickly enough.
(e) They are rushing down the aisles and getting in each other's way.
(f) Tell passengers to leave the aircraft.
(g) The exit next to you is out of action.
(h) Passengers must use the escape chute.

2 *Now practise giving these orders yourself.*

Useful words and phrases summary

drop in temperature
drop in pressure
depressurisation
touchdown
raft
mast
deck
steep dive
controlled descent
oxygen mask
forced landing

swift evacuation
ditching
escape chute
life raft
Brace for impact/Heads down
Evacuate now
single/double file
Breathe normally
Adjust the strap
Secure the table
Refer to the card

UNIT 9

FIRST AID

MEDICAL SUPPLIES

Reading

Read the text and do the exercise.

The airlines of many countries issue a CA with an individual kit for first aid. It typically contains:

mild pain killers	antiseptic cream or liquid
mild anti-travel sickness tablets	anti-malaria tablets
indigestion tablets	eye drops
cotton wool	nose drops
adhesive dressing (plasters)	

Every airliner must carry at least one sealed metal box known as a drugs kit. This typically contains:

collapsible splints	eye drops
scalpel	nose drops
drugs	a range of antiseptics
tranquillisers	a wide range of dressings
heart stimulants	

The captain must be consulted before breaking the seal of the drugs kit. In any case of medical treatment, the purser should be kept informed by the CA of the patient's condition.

Medical training is given to CAs by an airline, but for reasons of communication the CA needs to be familiar with English terminology. Diagnosing an illness or assessing an injury is based on the signs and symptoms of a patient. Signs are things which can be seen, such as swelling, external bleeding etc. Symptoms are things which the patient can feel but which cannot be seen: headache, pain, for example. Symptoms can only be

First Aid 89

established by the use of language. Language is also essential for giving instructions to a patient.

1 *Describe the sorts of things you would expect to find in a typical first aid kit.*

2 *What is the main difference between a first aid kit and a drugs kit?*

3 *Why is it important that you can communicate in English about illnesses?*

THE BODY

Label these two diagrams with the English names for the parts of the body. Use a bilingual dictionary if necessary.

What English words concerning pain are appropriate to use for each part of the body?

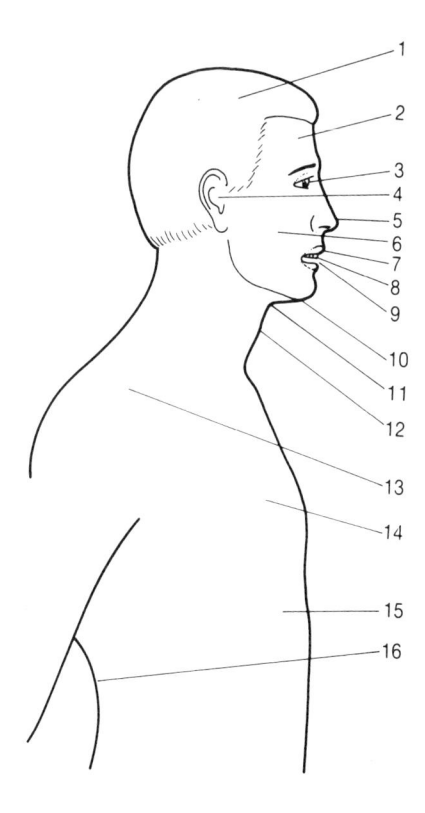

Consider what might be wrong if a passenger complained of pain in these parts of his body.

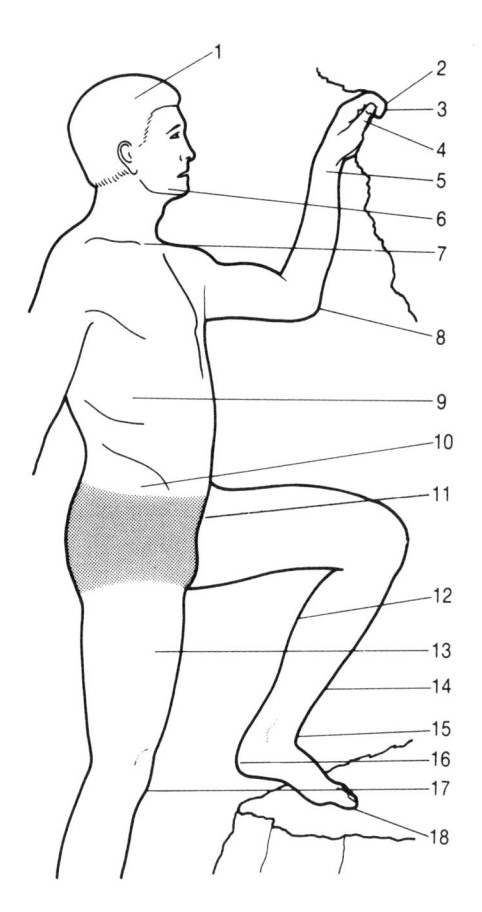

Although each CA is responsible for a particular part of the airliner, he or she has a general responsibility for the welfare of all passengers.

First Aid

INITIAL ENQUIRIES

Listening 1

Listen and repeat the model enquiries about passengers' well-being.

Listening 2

Listen to the passengers' statements about how they feel and complete the information.

	Symptoms
1.	
2.	
3.	
4.	
5.	
6.	
7.	
8.	
9.	
10.	

Language practice

Study the following ways of expressing illness:

I am feeling	a bit	ill
	a little	unwell
	slightly	
	rather	
	very	
	terribly	

(Note the differing degrees of discomfort)

| I have
I have got | a | slight
sharp
bit of a | pain
ache | in my | arm
chest
head
eyes
legs
stomach
back
throat |
|---|---|---|---|---|---|
| I feel | sick
dizzy
faint
ill
awful
hot
cold
feverish | | | | |

Note: 'I feel sick' in British English use means 'I may vomit'. 'Sick' in American English use usually means 'ill'.

1 *Match the most appropriate responses with the passengers' symptoms.*

Symptoms   **Responses**

I've got terrible toothache   Would you like me to get you an aspirin?
I feel very sick   Is there anything I can get you for it?
I feel very strange   Do you think you can make it to the toilet?
I've a pain in my chest   Would you like a glass of water or some
I'm feeling very dizzy/giddy   more air?
I've got a sore throat   What exactly are the symptoms?
I've got a pain   Where exactly?
There's been an accident   What happened?

2 *Match the likely action or medication with the symptoms.*

Symptoms		Action/medication	
headache	faint	sickness bag	call for doctor
toothache	too hot	aspirin	antacid tablet
chest pain	too cold	increase air flow	oxygen
indigestion	fever	plaster or dressing	blanket
cut	desire to vomit	smelling salts	
bruise			

3 *In pairs practise exchanges between passengers feeling ill and CAs giving assistance.*

First Aid

GETTING TO KNOW THE ILLNESSES

It is always important, in cases of more serious or prolonged passenger discomfort, to establish their medical history. For this you should be able to recognise certain conditions the passenger may mention. Complete the table below using a bilingual dictionary.

English	Your language
AIDS	
angina	
asthma	
diabetes	
dyspepsia	
epilepsy	
heart condition	
malaria	
migraine	
ulcer	

Calling for a doctor

In more serious cases, the purser or the captain may authorise a PA announcement to see whether there is a doctor on board. You should learn the following short announcement by heart.

Ladies and gentlemen.
Your attention please.
If there is a doctor on board, will he or she please contact a member of the cabin crew.
This is a request for a doctor.
Thank you.

Language practice

One student gives instructions to a 'patient' and the other student does what he is told. Give the instructions:

(a) as they are, in the case of emergency.
(b) prefixed by 'I want you to ...' for serious cases.
(c) prefixed by 'I'd like you to ...' for less serious cases.

Keep still	Wiggle your toes
Lean back in your seat	Bend your knee
Hold your head back	Turn on your side
Raise your arm	Lie down
Breathe deeply	Undo your collar
Tell me if you can feel anything (*touches patient*)	Loosen your belt

Your tone of voice must be firm, but gentle and encouraging. Discuss together:

- What would you say to a child patient?
- What can you say to reassure a very distressed patient?
- Where could a patient lie down most conveniently?
- Are there occasions when a patient should not be moved?

UNIT 10

ADDITIONAL ANNOUNCEMENTS

DELAYS

Apology for delayed take-off

Listening 1

Listen to the announcement and complete the missing words.

We _____ like to _____ the delay in taking off today.
_____ was _____ by _____ weather conditions at Lisbon airport.

Language practice

Practise making similar announcements using the following cue words.

1. minor technical problems/Frankfurt
2. heavy air traffic/London
3. ground staff problems/Sao Paulo
4. late arrival/connecting flight
5. bad weather/Barcelona

Punctuality and onward flights

If the flight is likely to arrive early or late, the captain himself will make an announcement, or ask the purser to do so. Passengers will of course ask anyway!

Study the exchanges overleaf:

Passenger question	CA response
Do you think we'll be in on time?	We are expecting a slight tail-wind today, sir, so we may arrive early.
Will we arrive on schedule?	Quite strong head-winds were forecast, madam, so there is a slight possibility of a late arrival.
Are we going to be late into Kinshasa?	We should arrive on schedule, sir/madam.

A passenger worried about a puntual arrival may be advised:

    I'll check with the captain, sir.

If there is going to be difficulty in catching a connecting flight, it may be necessary to say:

    I'll ask the captain to radio ahead, madam.

Practise, in pairs, a CA reassuring a passenger.

[Cartoon: Travel agent to just-married couple: "If you take into account the usual delays, you can spend the last four nights of your honeymoon in Majorca and the first three nights at Heathrow!"]

Passengers need to know about delays as they may have to change their plans.

Additional Announcements 97

ABORTED DEPARTURE

Language practice

While every effort is made to avoid the situation in which passengers have boarded an airliner which is then unable to take off, it can happen and an announcement must be made. Its content will depend on whether the aircraft has moved off from its position on the apron and whether delay or cancellation is planned.

Practise announcements making selections as appropriate:

Ladies and gentlemen.
We very much regret to inform you that due to:

deteriorating weather conditions heavy air traffic ground handling difficulties	at Riyadh airport,

minor technical problems,

we are unable to take off as scheduled.	we are returning to the apron.

Our flight will therefore be:

delayed for 15 minutes.	delayed until further notice.	cancelled.

A further announcement will be made:

shortly.	in the airport lounge.

We do apologise for this occurrence, which is beyond our control, and thank you for your understanding and patience.

Note: Passengers generally want further information from CAs. If the problem relates to the destination airport, all available information should have been given in the announcement. In the example, if it is known that sandstorms are the cause of the temporary closure of Riyadh airport, for instance, the phrase 'deteriorating weather conditions' should be replaced by 'sandstorms'. Do not, however, speculate. In the case of 'minor technical problems', it may be better not to give details even if you know them.

You should tell passengers who enquire:

> I'm sorry, sir. That's all the information we have at present.
> I'm very sorry, madam. We'll let you know as soon as we have some more information.

Passengers may also seek this reassurance:

> An announcement will be made at Riyadh airport and anyone waiting for the arrival of this flight will be kept informed.

TURBULENCE ANNOUNCEMENT

The captain himself will often make the announcement about turbulence, but you should be able to take over if required:

Ladies and gentlemen.
Your captain advises that we are approaching an area in which air turbulence may be experienced.
For your comfort, you are therefore kindly requested to remain seated with your seat belt fastened until the 'fasten seatbelt' sign is switched off.
Thank you.

Learn this by heart.

PASSENGER IDENTIFICATION ANNOUNCEMENT

Language practice

For various reasons, it may be necessary for the cabin crew to ask a particular passenger to identify himself/herself.

Ladies and gentlemen.
May I have your attention please.
Would *Mr Neil James* please identify *him*self to a member of the cabin crew.
That's *Mr Neil James* please.
Thank you.

Practise with the following people:

(a) Miss Hayat Anawis
(b) Mr Bruno Sauzier
(c) Herr Heribert Strobl

Additional Announcements

(d) Madamoiselle Françoise Induni
(e) The leader of the group from Churcher's College
(f) The captain of the Girdlers' Ladies Hockey Team
(g) Mr Jack Storie and Mr Mike Stanford

DIVERSION ANNOUNCEMENT

Listening 2

Listen to the announcement and complete the information. Repeat the whole announcement.

Ladies and gentlemen.
We very much regret to inform you that due to _____ at _____ , we are _____ to _____ .
We expect to land _____ minutes.
A further announcement will be made after landing.

Language practice

Make similar announcements using the following key words:

1. minor technical problems/returning/Mexico City/45 minutes
2. medical condition/passenger/landing/Brussels/20 minutes
3. thunderstorms/Detroit/diverting/Chicago/50 minutes
4. fog/Melbourne/diverting/Sydney/one hour
5. minor technical problems/landing/Kuwait/15 minutes

LANDING CARD ANNOUNCEMENT

Reading

Read this typical announcement and do the exercises.

We shall shortly begin distributing landing cards for passengers who do not hold passports issued by the United Kingdom.
Such passengers should complete the form using a ball-point pen and in capital letters.
Please keep the completed landing card with your passport for presentation to immigration officers after landing.
Thank you.

Prepare the information needed below for a passenger.

Then, in pairs, role play a CA and a passenger with limited English who needs help in filling in a landing card.

LANDING CARD
Immigration Act 1971

Please complete clearly in BLOCK CAPITALS
Veuillez remplir lisiblement en LETTRES MAJUSCULES
Bitte deutlich in DRUCKSCHRIFT ausfüllen

Family name
Nom de famille
Familienname ....

Forenames
Prénoms
Vornamen ....

Sex (M,F)
Sexe
Geschlecht ____

Date of birth Day Month Year
Date de naissance
Geburtsdatum

Place of birth
Lieu de naissance
Geburtsort ....

Nationality
Nationalité
Staatsangehörigkeit ....

Occupation
Profession
Beruf ....

Address in United Kingdom
Adresse en Royaume Uni
Adresse im Vereinigten Königreich ....

Signature
Signature
Unterschrift ....

BC 692 486

For offical use/ Reserve usage officiel /Nur für den Dienstgebrauch

CAT ____ -16 ____ CODE ____ NAT ____ POL ____

IS28FG

Additional Announcements

DELAYED LANDING ANNOUNCEMENT

Language practice

Using the model below, practise making similar announcements with your own situations:

We regret to inform you that due to

| heavy air traffic
temporary weather conditions | at *Manila* Airport. |

our landing will be delayed by approximately *20 minutes*.
Thank you.

Useful words and phrases summary

delay
connecting
operational difficulties
minor technical problems
heavy air traffic (congestion)
ground staff problems

as scheduled
until further notice
turbulence
We would like to apologise for ...
We very much regret to inform
 you that ...
May I have your attention please.
You are kindly requested to ...

UNIT 11

LANDING, TRANSIT AND DISEMBARKATION

DESCENT

Language practice

At the start of the descent for landing, the captain switches on the 'fasten seatbelt' sign. To the CAs, this is a sign to begin the descent procedure. They must check that:

(a) passengers have fastened their seatbelts
(b) tables are securely stowed
(c) seat backs are upright
(d) luggage racks are closed
(e) food and service trolleys are stowed
(f) the flight deck is clear of meal trays etc.

Can you remember what to say in these situations?

Practise making announcements and instructing passengers.

DESCENT ANNOUNCEMENT

Language practice

The following announcement is made at the start of the descent:

Ladies and gentlemen.
We are now commencing our descent to Athens Airport.
You are kindly requested to fasten your seatbelt, put your seat in the fully upright position and fold your tray table upright into the seat in front of you.
Thank you.

Practise saying this announcement until you are word perfect.

Landing, Transit and Disembarkation

FINAL APPROACH

Language practice

The start of the final approach to landing is indicated by the captain switching on the 'no smoking' sign. When CAs see this and/or hear the tone associated with it, they take their seats and fasten their safety belts. At this stage on a night flight, the CAs are responsible for turning down the level of cabin lighting.

The following announcement is made:

Ladies and gentlemen.
The captain has now switched on the 'no smoking' sign.
Would you please extinguish all cigarettes and check that your seat belts are securely fastened for landing.
Thank you.

As with taking off, it is essential that passengers comply with safety regulations during the final approach. Each CA should watch that passengers do so.

CAs must remain seated until the aircraft turns at the end of the runway after landing. On a night flight, a CA would turn up the level of cabin lighting at this point.

Practise the announcement until you are word perfect.

AFTER-LANDING ANNOUNCEMENT

Listening 1

This announcement usually includes details of the weather at the airport and the local time. It should always include a 'thank you' from the airline.

Listen to the model announcement and complete the information:

Place of arrival:

Weather:

Temperature:

Local time:

Language practice

Practise making similar announcements using the following cue words. If you already work for an airline, use your airline's name.

1. Vienna, windy, 21, 7.30, Austrian Airlines
2. Jeddah, hot, 36, 2.20, Saudia
3. Buenos Aires, cloudy, 15, 8.45, Aerolineas Argentinas
4. Edinburgh, warm, 67°F, 11.35, Air UK
5. Belgrade, rainy, 23°C, 6.10, Yugoslav Airlines

TRANSIT VARIATIONS

Language practice

Notice the difference in meaning of the word 'transit' when talking about transit passengers and a transit stop.

A transit passenger is one who is taking a different, onward flight.
A transit stop means that the airliner is continuing to a further destination.

For a transit stop, an addition to the last announcement is necessary. It may take one of three forms:

Passengers staying with us for the flight to Tokyo are kindly requested to:

(A) disembark, taking all their hand baggage with them for passport and customs control.

(ONE of these variations.)

(B) disembark. Hand baggage may be left on board.

(C) remain on board. Please note that smoking is not allowed while the 'no smoking' sign is on.

We shall continue our flight to Tokyo in 50 minutes.

1 *Practise these variations as follows:*

(a) Cologne, C, 15 minutes.
(b) Kinshasa, A, 45 minutes.
(c) Muscat, B, 30 minutes.
(d) Singapore, B, 1 hour.
(e) Brazilia, A, 50 minutes.

2 *Why do you think the cabin lighting is turned down on a night flight?*

3 *Why do you think CAs have to remain seated until after the aircraft turns at the end of the runway?*

Landing, Transit and Disembarkation 105

TAXYING AND DISEMBARKATION

Language practice

Unfortunately passengers often unfasten their seatbelts and move towards the exits as soon as the plane has turned off the runway. They perhaps think that it is safe to do so because they see CAs moving to their disembarkation positions. The following brief announcement may be necessary:

Ladies and gentlemen.
May I remind you that, for safety reasons, you should remain in your seats with seatbelts fastened until the plane has come to a complete rest.
Thank you for your co-operation.

Once the aircraft has come to a complete rest, CAs must ensure that stairs or airbridges are properly positioned before allowing disembarkation. In some aircraft, the stairs are self-contained.
Sometimes passengers have to leave the aircraft by exits different from those used for boarding. The following announcement can be made:

Ladies and gentlemen.
You are kindly requested to leave the aircraft by the front/side/rear door(s) only.
Thank you.

Why do you think this can happen?

Reading

As passengers disembark, the following expressions are appropriate:

> Goodbye, sir/madam.
> We hope you enjoyed your flight.
> Thank you for flying (with) Alitalia.

If a nearby jet starts up during disembarkation or turns on the apron, the cabin crew should halt disembarkation until the problem stops.
   Finally, CAs must ensure that passengers with medical problems (such as wheelchair or stretcher cases) are safely disembarked, and that any UMs are handed over to an appropriate member of the airline's (or its agent's) passenger handling ground services staff.
   During a transit stop, the cabin crew remain aboard to ensure that safety instructions, in particular the no smoking rule, are obeyed. Doors should be kept closed, but unlocked, if the stairs do not have to be moved to open them. CAs must ensure that the following on-ground routines are observed:

(a) clear access along aisles and to doors,
(b) cabin partition curtains open and held back.

Passengers may walk around.

If refuelling is taking place, CAs must be vigilant for a sign of fuel vapour escaping into the cabin. They must remain in the part of the cabin to which they have been assigned. The legal minimum number of CAs must remain on board during transit stops.

Recap questions

1. What are the three checks that directly involve passengers which must be made at the start of descent?
2. Name the checks to be made at the same time which do not directly involve passengers.
3. When does a CA on a night flight adjust the cabin lighting level?
4. Explain the different use of the word 'transit' in the expressions 'transit passenger' and 'transit stop'.
5. What are the three possible actions for passengers during a transit stop?
6. Outline the role of cabin crew during a transit stop.

Useful words and phrases summary

transit
disembark
refuelling

May I remind you ...
Thank you for flying (with) ...

APPENDIX A
FINAL TEST

TESTING PROCEDURE

The final test requires spoken answers which should be recorded on to a cassette, preferably in a language laboratory. If no language laboratory is available the test should be conducted using two cassette recorders — one playing the test cassette and the other recording the candidate's response. If only one cassette is available, it should be used to play the recorded test, and a teacher should mark the responses as they are spoken. Marking of the responses should be done by a qualified and experienced teacher of English as a foreign language. Students will need paper and pencil in order to write down details to be used in the second part of the test. Teachers are strongly recommended to give the test a dummy run in order to familiarise themselves with the requirements of stopping and starting tape recorders. The test is in three parts:

(1) Terminology (10 marks)

In this first section, ten explanations of words or phrases are given. The candidate has to identify each word and say it.

(2) Announcements (30 marks)

Candidates are required to make six announcements. The first two are longer, standard announcements and are given below. The second four are shorter, spontaneous announcements that a purser might ask a CA to make. The prompts for these four announcements are given on the cassette, but the script for them is not included in the tapescript printed in the book. Prompts for the first two are also given on the cassette, so that the six announcements can be tested consecutively.

(3) Interaction with passengers (60 marks)

Fifteen situations are given to which the CA must respond.

MARKING

(Read in conjunction with the marking sheet which is designed to be photocopied.)

(1) Terminology

The answers carry one mark each, and pronunciation may be ignored so long as the word is clearly recognisible.

(2) Announcements

(a) The first two announcements are scored on a scale of 0 to 5 in the following three categories:

  (i) Pronunciation/accent
  Criteria: To what extent is comprehensibility affected by bad pronunciation at a phonemic level?
  To what extent does the candidate betray his/her mother tongue?

  (ii) Stress, rhythm, intonation
  Criteria: To what extent does the candidate maintain suitable stress?
  To what extent is the intention of the announcement conveyed by voice tone?

  (iii) Catenation/juncture
  Criteria: To what extent does the candidate run words together and keep words separate correctly?

The scores for each announcement are added together and divided by three.

(b) The second four announcements are scored as above, but with the addition of two further categories, the criteria for which are self-explanatory:

  Content
  Grammatical accuracy

The scores for each of these announcements are added together and divided by five.

(3) Interaction with passengers

These responses are each scored on a scale of 0 to 4 to the following guidelines:

  0 Candidate fails to respond. Candidate's response is likely to be misunderstood or misinterpreted by an average native speaker.

Appendix A

1 A response, no matter how unaccurately produced, that makes the candidate understood.
2 A response that is comprehensible and reasonably appropriate although with quite serious faults.
3 Appropriate, comprehensible and unambiguous; there may be faults in several aspects of production, but these will not be serious.
4 Appropriate, readily comprehensible, unambiguous; only exceptionally minor faults.

The scores for each announcement are added together.

ESTABLISHING AN APPROPRIATE PASS LEVEL

The appropriate pass level will depend upon:

(a) the airline's needs in general;
(b) the average level of candidates;
(c) whether CAs are being selected for domestic routes, international multilingual routes or international routes involving countries with English as the lingua franca.

The individual airline is therefore best equipped to select its own pass level(s). However, the following offers very generalised guidelines.

Domestic route with largely native-speaking passengers	55%, with more than half marks in each section.
International route with significant numbers of English-speaking passengers	80%

The format of the test allows the English language training unit of an airline to generate further standardised tests.

NAME: _____ DATE: _____

THANK YOU FOR FLYING WITH US

FINAL TEST

MARKING SHEET

(1) Terminology

1 2 3 4 5 6 7 8 9 10   Sub-total: _____

(2) Announcements

1. Pronunciation/accent   0 1 2 3 4 5
   Stress, rhythm, intonation 0 1 2 3 4 5
   Catenation/juncture   0 1 2 3 4 5
   Score (/15)   = _____ ÷ 3 = _____

2. Pronunciation/accent   0 1 2 3 4 5
   Stress, rhythm, intonation 0 1 2 3 4 5
   Catenation/juncture   0 1 2 3 4 5
   Score (/15)   = _____ ÷ 5 = _____

3. Pronunciation/accent   0 1 2 3 4 5
   Stress, rhythm, intonation 0 1 2 3 4 5
   Catenation/junction   0 1 2 3 4 5
   Content   0 1 2 3 4 5
   Grammatical accuracy   0 1 2 3 4 5
   Score (/25)   = _____ ÷ 5 = _____

4. Pronunciation/accent   0 1 2 3 4 5
   Stress, rhythm, intonation 0 1 2 3 4 5
   Catenation/juncture   0 1 2 3 4 5
   Content   0 1 2 3 4 5
   Grammatical accuracy   0 1 2 3 4 5
   Score (/25)   = _____ ÷ 5 = _____

5. Pronunciation/accent   0 1 2 3 4 5
   Stress, rhythm, intonation 0 1 2 3 4 5
   Catenation/juncture   0 1 2 3 4 5
   Content   0 1 2 3 4 5
   Grammatical accuracy   0 1 2 3 4 5
   Score (/25)   = _____ ÷ 5 = _____

Appendix A

6. Pronunciation/accent	0	1	2	3	4	5
Stress, rhythm, intonation	0	1	2	3	4	5
Catenation/juncture	0	1	2	3	4	5
Content	0	1	2	3	4	5
Grammatical accuracy	0	1	2	3	4	5

Score (/25) = _____ ÷ 5 = _____

Sub-total: _____

(3) Interaction with passengers

1. 0 1 2 3 4
2. 0 1 2 3 4
3. 0 1 2 3 4
4. 0 1 2 3 4
5. 0 1 2 3 4
6. 0 1 2 3 4
7. 0 1 2 3 4
8. 0 1 2 3 4
9. 0 1 2 3 4
10. 0 1 2 3 4
11. 0 1 2 3 4
12. 0 1 2 3 4
13. 0 1 2 3 4
14. 0 1 2 3 4
15. 0 1 2 3 4

Sub-Total: _____

Grand total: _____%

APPENDIX B
GETTING A JOB AS A CA

The first line of approach is to write to your local airline, addressing your letter to the personnel officer. You will receive general information regarding their minimum requirements for accepting a trainee. These will generally include restrictions regarding:

    Age
    Height
    Health and physical fitness
    Swimming ability
    General education
    Foreign language ability, particularly with regard to English

Be warned that the number of people seeking places is greatly in excess of the number of places available; in some countries there are more than 20 applicants for each place.

To improve your chances of being selected, you may wish to consider undertaking, at your own expense, a basic cabin crew course, involving English language training as offered in this book, as appropriate. Details of such a course can be obtained from:

    Director of Educational Services,
    Air Service Training Ltd.,
    Perth Aerodrome,
    Perth PH2 6NPB,
    United Kingdom.

This course does not in itself lead to an employment opportunity, but successful completion of it demonstrates to an airline that an applicant has a basic understanding and knowledge of the job, and proven motivation.

TAPESCRIPT

UNIT 2: BOARDING

Listening 1

CAPT: ... and so I'll ask David Nokes, our cabin services manager for today's flight to continue with *his* briefing.

CSM: Thank you Captain Lockhart. Well, as the captain has informed you, we are bound for Vienna on a Boeing 757 and flight time is 2 hours and 20 minutes.

That means we'll be serving dinner, with full silver service in the first class, so you'll need to watch the time. I'll take the first class with you, Mike, and Lynda, you'll be steward for business and economy classes, assisted by Jochem, Peter and Sandra.

We have 15 checked in to first class, 24 in business and 63 in economy. That's a relatively light loading so we should manage all services in time.

There are three UMs, two sisters and a brother, aged seven, five and four. I'd like you, Sandra, to take responsibility for them. There's one CIP, a Dr Schindler of Austrian Airlines, travelling first class.

We have a Mr and Mrs Turner travelling economy, who've ordered vegetarian meals.

Jochem, I'd like you to make announcements, English and German, please.

Now, before I assign specific cabin areas, we'll run through safety procedures and equipment on the 757.

Sandra, where are the emergency exits located ...

Listening 2

1. Good morning, ladies and gentlemen.
   Aer Lingus flight no. EIN151 to Dublin is now ready for boarding. Passengers for this flight should proceed now through the door at the end of the departure lounge. Please extinguish all smoking material before leaving this lounge. Thank you.
2. Boarding will take place according to the seat numbers shown on the boarding cards. You are asked not to proceed through the gate until these numbers are called. Thank you.
3. Economy class passengers holding boarding cards with seat numbers between rows 15 and 25 are requested to board now. Thank you.

Listening 3

A. Don't worry madam. Let me help you.
B. Let me see, 27C. Right here and you'll find it at the end on the left.
C. Flight time is about 6 hours.

D. Yes, this is the flight to Frankfurt.
E. Don't worry sir, I'm sure you'll have an enjoyable flight.
F. Good morning, madam; welcome on board.
G. The flight conditions are reported as favourable. There's really no need to worry.
H. You have a special seat allocated to make feeding easier. Your cabin attendant will be with you as soon as we have taken off.
I. Is there anything I can do to help you madam?
J. I'm sorry. Please put that cigarette out immediately.

Listening 4
A. I'm sorry. Smoking is not allowed. Please extinguish your cigarette.
B. Can I see both your boarding cards please?
C. Excuse me, but I think you may be in the wrong seat. Can I see your boarding card?
D. Excuse me, but you should be in the economy cabin.
E. I'm afraid you can't change seats but if you like, I'll ask the passenger in the window seat if she would mind changing.
F. I'm sorry, but this seat is for a member of the cabin crew. Can I see your boarding card?
G. Let me help you. Can I see your boarding card?

Listening 5
1. CA: Can I help you?
   PASS: I can't get my rucksack into the overhead compartment.
   CA: Don't worry. If you'd like to sit down, I'll do it for you.
2. CA: Excuse me.
   PASS: Yes?
   CA: I'm afraid you can't leave your bag there.
   PASS: Why not? It's not in anyone's way.
   CA: No, but it might be. You're sitting next to the emergency exit.
   PASS: So where do I put it? I'll need things in it during the flight.
   CA: I think you'll find there's enough room to put it under your seat.
3. CA: Would you like me to stow your briefcase somewhere else? You don't look very comfortable with it there by your feet.
   PASS: Thank you.
4. PASS: I'm not sure what to do with my coat.
   CA: If you leave it with me, I'll hang it in the wardrobe compartment.
5. PASS: I was told I could bring this suitcase into the cabin with me, but it's too big to go in the compartment or under the seat.
   CA: Well, if you'd like to let me take it, I'll look after it for you.

Listening 6
Good morning, ladies and gentlemen. On behalf of Captain Al-Hassani and his crew, I would like to welcome you aboard Gulf Air flight no. GFA357 to Bahrain. Our flight to Bahrain will take 90 minutes and we shall be flying at a height of 35 000 feet. You are kindly requested to fasten your seatbelts, put your seat backs in the fully upright position and, please, pay attention to the 'no smoking' sign. Please note that smoking in the toilets is forbidden at all times. We advise that you keep your seatbelt fastened throughout the flight. On behalf of Captain Al-Hassani and his crew, I wish you a pleasant flight. Thank you.

Listening 7
Ladies and gentlemen.
Our cabin pressure is controlled for your comfort, but should it change at anytime during the flight, an oxygen mask will automatically fall from the unit above your seat. If this

happens, please extinguish your cigarette immediately, pull down the mask and place it firmly over your mouth and nose. Secure the mask with the strap, as the cabin attendants are demonstrating. Continue to breath normally, until you are advised that the oxygen masks are no longer required. A detailed safety instruction card may be found in the seat pocket in front of you.

Listening 8
Ladies and gentlemen.
As part of our flight today is over water, international regulations require that we demonstrate the use of the life jacket. Each passenger is provided with a life jacket which is located beneath your seat. Your cabin crew is now demonstrating how to use it.
Pull the life jacket over your head.
Fasten the jacket with the tapes around your waist as the crew are now demonstrating.
Do NOT, repeat NOT, inflate the jacket until you have left the aircraft.
The jacket is automatically inflated by pulling these tags, or, if necessary, by blowing into this tube.
A light is provided here, and a whistle for attracting attention.
Thank you for listening.

UNIT 3: TAKE-OFF AND INITIAL FLIGHT

Listening 1

Summary of CA duties
Now, before the aircraft even moves off the ramp, there are a number of things you need to check. For example, the passengers need to be checked. You must make sure that none of them is smoking. You've got to check that seats are upright. There's always one who's forgotten! Another thing to check at the same time is that all seatbelts are fastened. You need to be especially careful with this as passengers often put papers on their laps, or they pull their coats round their waists. So, if you can't tell by just looking, you've got to ask.

Another thing to watch for with seatbelts is the problem of passengers who are carrying a young child or a baby. If they're carrying the child inside the seatbelt, they've got to either put the child outside the belt and hold onto the child with their hands, or you can get the passenger a supplementary seatbelt.

You've got cabin equipment checks to make as well. Check that all the galley equipment is properly secured. It could be rather nasty if a trolley suddenly rushed through the cabin during take-off! Check that all the luggage compartments are properly shut, and that the doors and curtains are open. And last but not least keep an eye out for the passengers' tables. There's always somebody who'll forget and lower it again.

UNIT 4: FOOD AND DRINK

Listening 1
PASSENGER 1: Excuse me, I never eat a cooked breakfast. Could I have a continental one?
2: What is lamb biryani?
3: My daughter is not a big eater. Have you something smaller I can give her?
4: Please, I do not eat pork.
5: Some more bread, please.

Listening 2
1. I'm starving. What's on the menu?
2. What is californienne?
3. No meat for me. What do you recommend?
4. I'm allergic to eggs. Is there anything I should avoid?
5. I can't stand garlic.
6. A light dessert, please.
7. No me like fish.

Listening 3
Would you like some soup, sir?
Can I help you to some sauce?
A little dressing, madam?
Would you like some soup, madam, or would you prefer the hors d'oeuvres?
We have Wiener Schnitzel or Dover sole mornay for the main course.
Which would you prefer madam?
We can offer you fresh fruit salad with cream or perhaps you would like gateau.
Tea or coffee, sir?
Black or white, madam?
May I take your soup bowl, sir?
Have you finished your hors d'oeuvres, madam?
Is there something wrong, sir?
Did you enjoy your beef, sir?
How was the chicken?

Listening 4
A. Scotch on the rocks
B. Something long and non-alcoholic
C. Johnny Walker
D. Bourbon
E. A tonic
F. Vodka tonic
G. Bloody Mary
H. Bucks Fizz
I. Screwdriver
J. Irish coffee
K. Shandy
L. Rum and Coke

Listening 5
... OK I'll just give you an idea of what exactly this galley consists of. Right up on the top left you'll see the tape player. The cupboard directly under it holds the hot and cold liquid containers. You can see the dispensers sticking out of the bottom, and the drip tray beneath. The other cupboard is for storage, and beneath that is the head-rest for the seat. Notice the work light just to the left of it. Well, this is obviously the seat, beneath the head-rest, but you probably wouldn't guess that behind the seat are the ice containers! These two cupboards down on the right are for storage, and the one on the bottom left is the locked drinks locker. The big one above it has a waste bin in the top, and drinks at the bottom. Right?

UNIT 5: IN-FLIGHT ENTERTAINMENT

Listening 1
A member of the crew usually makes an announcement about the films being shown. Listen to the following typical announcement and then try it yourself, repeating if necessary.

Ladies and gentlemen.
We shall shortly begin our feature film which we hope you will enjoy watching. Today's film is entitled *Return to Errol*, a drama starring Lindsay Horne, David Tough and Jack Herd. Headsets are obtainable from the cabin crew, and the English sound track of *Return to Errol* is on channel 1 for the first class cabin and channel 2 for economy class.

Tapescript

Music is available on the other channels and details are given in the *In-Flight Magazine*, which may be found in the pocket of the seat in front of you. International regulations require us to make a charge for the hire of the headset. If you would like to change your seat, please inform a member of the cabin crew.
Thank you.

UNIT 6: DUTY FREE SALES

Listening 1
Ladies and gentlemen.
We shall shortly commence the sale of duty-free goods. Full details of our selection of cigarettes, spirits, perfumes and other items are given in the *In-Flight Magazine* which you will find in the seat pocket in front of you.
On today's flight we can accept French francs, pounds Sterling and dollars. Travellers cheques and major credit cards are also accepted.
May we point out that our rates of exchange are company rates which are not necessarily the current bank rates.
Thank you.

Listening 2
Ladies and gentlemen. We have on board today a fine selection of duty-free goods. We have Miss Dior eau du toilette, and as perfumes we are carrying Channel No. 5 and White Linen. For gentlemen we have Aramis aftershave. For gifts, a selection of silk ties and scarves is available. We can offer you Scotch whisky, gin and vodka, and a selection of cigars and cigarettes.
We can accept payment in Swiss francs or US dollars, but we regret that change can only be given in Swiss francs. American Express and Diners Club charge cards, and also Visa and Mastercard credit cards are accepted.
Thank you.

Listening 3
1. A. Can I have a small bottle of Agua di Silva?
   B. I am sorry sir, we don't have that brand.
2. A. A bottle of Chanel No. 5 please. The spray.
   B. I'm sorry, madam, we have sold out I think. We can only carry a limited stock of each item and this one has been very popular today.
3. A. Can you recommend a perfume for a young girl?
   B. What sort of price did you have in mind?
4. A. I want to buy something for a man who doesn't smoke or drink.
   B. How about a silk tie?
5. A. Can I pay in dollars travellers cheques?
   B. Of course, madam.
6. A. I'm so sorry to trouble you but could you get me a bottle of L'Air du Temps.
   B. Of course. It's no trouble at all.

UNIT 7

Listening 1
1. There seems to be a fuel leak on that wing. Look!
2. What is that roaring sound?
3. It's terribly bumpy. Is there anything wrong?
4. That wing seems to be coming apart!
5. What aircraft is this, again?
6. Will we be able to land in this storm?

Listening 2
1. A. Do you think I'll need a coat when we land?
   B. I don't think so, madam. It's still quite warm in Barcelona at this time of year.
2. A. Will I be all right in this dress or do you think I should put a cardigan on?
   B. Well, you never know. Perhaps it would be safer to wear a cardigan.
3. A. Is it easy to get a hotel booking in Kuwait?
   B. You shouldn't have any problem at this time of year.
4. A. How am I going to get into the city?
   B. You can take a taxi or the information desk in the terminal building will be able to advise you about public transport.
5. A. I have a connecting flight to San Antonio. Any idea what I should do?
   B. Yes, sir. When we get to Dallas, you enquire at the transfer desk.
6. A. Any idea what the weather's like in Rome?
   B. I'm not sure but the captain will announce the weather conditions just before we land.

Listening 3
1. A: What is the local time in Cairo now?
   B: They are two hours ahead, so it's 3.20, sir.
2. A: What time is it in London?
   B: One hour behind, so it's 4.15, sir.
3. A: What do I have to do to adjust my watch to New York time?
   B: Wind back 5 hours, madam.
4. A: Do I need to change my watch?
   B: Yes, sir. Put it one hour forward for Rome.
5. A: I've lost track completely. What time and what day is it?
   B: It's Wednesday 24th June and 2.15 in the morning.
   A: Well, I've got the right date on my watch, but it's showing 5.15 a.m.

Listening 4
1. Is there any other seat I could take to make it easier for my baby?
2. Could you possibly heat this bottle for me?
3. Could you fix the support for the cot, please?
4. You wouldn't happen to have any spare nappies, would you?
5. I can't seem to stop my baby crying; would you have anything I could give her?

Listening 5
A. I am very sorry sir, I'm going to have to ask you to stop using your personal stereo as it may interfere with the aircraft's electronic systems.
B. The captain will probably say no as we are flying through a very busy area, but I will ask him.
C. Hello. This is the steward. Is anything the matter?
D. I'm terribly sorry, sir, but you must stop. It's a matter of safety.
E. I'll have to check with the captain, madam, to see if it is possible. If it is, then I'm sure he'll say yes.

Listening 6
1. I've asked three times for a glass of water. How much longer do I have to wait?
2. My meal was stone cold!
3. I think the man sitting next to me has had too much to drink. He keeps bothering me.
4. Can't you do something to keep those children quiet?
5. Is there anything you can do about that screaming child. It hasn't stopped yelling since we took off.
6. The toilets are in a disgusting state.

Tapescript

7. I'm sitting in a no-smoking section and the man in front is smoking.
8. I asked for a no-smoking seat but there were none left. Now I can hardly breathe with the smoke everywhere.
9. I don't think much of your duty-free goods. You've got nothing that I want.
10. The service on this plane is terrible! I'll certainly never fly with you again.

UNIT 8: EMERGENCY PROCEDURES

Listening 1
Ladies and gentlemen.
Due to a loss of cabin pressure, we are making a rapid controlled descent for a few minutes to a safer altitude.
Please extinguish all cigarettes immediately. During this period, please use your oxygen mask. Pull it down, place it over your nose and mouth and breathe normally. Adjust the strap to secure the mask. Parents should adjust their own masks first, then assist their children. Please breathe through the masks until you are advised to remove them.
Thank you.

Listening 2
Ladies and gentlemen.
Please listen very carefully.
We have to make an emergency landing in approximately 15 minutes.
Your safety will depend on carrying out the following instructions carefully and calmly.
Your crew have been especially trained for situations of this nature.
Please remain seated, extinguish all cigarettes, place your seat in the upright position and secure the table in front of you.
Refer to the card in the seat pocket in front of you for details of emergency landing procedures.
Listen for the next announcement shortly.

Listening 3
Please remove your shoes, glasses, dentures, pens and all sharp objects which might injure you.
Put on your life jacket but do not, repeat not, inflate it until you have left the aircraft.
Fasten your seat belt as tightly as possible after placing a cushion or a coat between the safety belt and your body.
When you hear the command 'brace for impact' or the 'fasten seatbelt' sign starts to flash, take the position we are now showing you.
During the landing you will feel several sharp bumps.
Remain in the 'brace for impact' position with seatbelt fastened until the plane comes to a complete rest.
Wait for instructions before moving, and keep calm.

UNIT 9: FIRST AID

Listening 1
Are you feeling all right, sir?
Is anything the matter, madam?
Can I help you in any way?
Is something the matter, sir?
Can I be of any assistance, madam?
Is everything all right?

Listening 2
1. I've got a headache.
2. I've got a toothache.
3. I've got a slight pain in the chest.
4. My stomach is a bit upset.
5. I just don't feel too good.
6. I feel a little dizzy.
7. I think I'm going to throw up.
8. I've just caught my finger on the edge of the seat.
9. I'm feeling a bit hot.
10. I'm feeling rather sick.

UNIT 10: ADDITIONAL ANNOUNCEMENTS

Listening 1
We would like to apologise for the delay in taking off today. This was caused by unfavourable weather conditions at Lisbon airport.

Listening 2
Ladies and gentlemen.
We very much regret to inform you that due to heavy fog at Frankfurt Airport, we are diverting to Munich.
We expect to land in approximately 30 minutes.
A further announcement will be made after landing.

UNIT 11: LANDING, TRANSIT AND DISEMBARKATION

Listening 1
Ladies and gentlemen.
You are requested to remain seated with your seatbelts fastened until the aircraft has come to a full stop.
This request is made for your own safety.
The weather in Seoul is sunny, and the temperature is 28°. Local time is 3.15.
Please ensure that you take all your hand baggage with you when leaving the aircraft.
Passengers taking onward flights from Seoul are asked to report to the transit desk.
We hope you have enjoyed your flight with us today.
Thank you for flying Korean Airlines.

Tapescript

FINAL TEST TAPESCRIPT

Welcome to this test for *Thank You for Flying With Us*. You may not have taken a test in this way before, but it is a very simple way of doing tests.
 To let you know when you should speak, you will hear this tone. [*Ping*]

To make sure you understand before we start, you or your teacher should now stop your machine.

(STOP MASTER TAPE. Check students. START MASTER TAPE)
Good. The test is in three parts.

Part 1
The first part of this test is to see how good your knowledge of cabin crew vocabulary is. You will hear a description of a word or phrase and you must say what the word or phrase is.

Listen to this example:
> This is the pilot responsible for the aircraft. [*Ping*]
> > Captain.

Now you answer.

1. Where meals are heated and coffee prepared. [*Ping*]
2. A movable container which is pushed along the aisle. [*Ping*]
3. These are distributed to passengers so they can hear music or the film sound-track. [*Ping*]
4. The senior member of the cabin crew. [*Ping*]
5. This holds a passenger safely in his seat. [*Ping*]
6. This is used to leave the aircraft after an emergency landing. [*Ping*]
7. Passengers and crew sit in this after ditching. [*Ping*]
8. A nursing mother may want this to put her baby in. [*Ping*]
9. This is used by cabin crew to communicate with the flight deck. [*Ping*]
10. This is used after a forced landing for speaking to passengers. [*Ping*]

End of part 1.

Part 2
In part 2, we will be testing how good you are at making announcements.

Announcement 1

You must make an announcement to demonstrate the use of oxygen masks. Start your announcement with:

Ladies and gentlemen.
Our cabin pressure is controlled for your comfort ...
Begin your announcement now. [*Ping*]

Announcement 2

You must make an announcement to demonstrate the use of life jackets. Start your announcement with:

Ladies and gentlemen.
As part of our flight today is over water ...
Begin your announcement now. [*Ping*]

Announcement 3

Next we would like you to make a welcome announcement. Make a note of the following details:

> It is morning
> The captain is Captain Achour
> It is an Air Algerie flight
> The flight no. is DAH2055 to Algiers
> Flight time is 3 hours 30 minutes
> Cruising altitude is 33,000 feet

I will repeat the details.
(Repeat)
Begin your announcement now. [Ping]

Announcement 4

The purser wants you to make an announcement. He says, 'Look. Apparently there's heavy air traffic at Paris so we're returning to the apron. Let the passengers know we'll be delayed for 15 minutes and we'll make another announcement shortly, OK?'

Listen to what he says again.
(Repeat)
Now make the announcement. [Ping]

Announcement 5

The purser says, 'We're going to be about 30 minutes late into Singapore because of heavy rain. Let the passengers know please.'

Listen to what he says again.
(Repeat)
Now make the announcement. [Ping]

Announcement 6

For the final announcement, we'd like you to make an after-landing announcement. Make a note of the following details:

> You have just landed in Amsterdam.
> The weather is cloudy.
> The temperature is 14°.
> Local time is 18.35.
> Your airline is Lufthansa.

I will repeat the details.
(Repeat)
Now make the announcement. [Ping]

Part 3

In this final part, you will have to respond to passengers' queries and deal with particular situations with passengers. For some questions, you will be given extra information before the passenger makes his or her query.

Tapescript

Here is the first one:

1. Passengers are boarding the aircraft. One of them says, 'I can't remember my seat number.' What do you say? [*Ping*]
2. A passenger says, 'What should I do with my overcoat?' What do you say? [*Ping*]
3. A passenger lights a cigarette before take off. What do you say? [*Ping*]
4. A passenger looks bored. You decide to offer him a newspaper. What do you say? (*Ping*)
5. During take-off a passenger gets up from his seat. What do you say? [*Ping*]
6. You are serving pre-set meal trays. You can't reach to serve a tray to a passenger seated by the window. What do you say to the passenger in the aisle seat? [*Ping*]
7. A passenger complains. 'My fish is cold!' What do you say? [*Ping*]
8. You are serving drinks from the trolley. Offer one to a passenger. [*Ping*]
9. A passenger says, 'Excuse me. How do I turn my light on?' [*Ping*]
10. You are selling duty-free goods. A passenger says, 'I'd like some perfume for my wife, but I'm not sure what she'd like.' What would you suggest? [*Ping*]
11. A nervous passenger asks, 'How can it be safe to fly through all this cloud?' What would you say? [*Ping*]
12. A passenger asks, 'How can I get into Jeddah from the airport?' What would you say? [*Ping*]
13. You know that a request for a visit to the flight deck will be turned down by the captain because on this flight he has a very heavy work load. A passenger asks, 'Would it be possible to visit the flight deck?' What do you say? [*Ping*]
14. You see a passenger using a calculator, which is not allowed on the particular airliner you are working on. What do you say? [*Ping*]
15. You are concerned because a passenger has been in the toilet for a very long time. You knock on the door. What do you say? [*Ping*]

That is the end of the test.
Please do not move from your seat until the teacher tells you to.
Thank you.

GLOSSARY

ABP (n.) *See* able-bodied passenger.
Able-bodied passenger Passenger selected by CA to assist with the evacuation of the aircraft following a forced landing.
Airbridge (n.) Movable corridor brought up to the doors of an airliner.
Airline (n.) Company that transports passengers and/or cargo by air.
Airliner (n.) Aircraft for carrying large numbers of passengers.
Aisle (n.) Walkway between the seats along the length of an airliner.
Allocate (v.) Give out, distribute reservations, for example. Hence *allocation* (n.)
Approach (n.) The final part of a flight, nearing the destination.
Apron (n.) The part of an airport where airliners park after arrival and before departure. Also known as 'ramp' (q.v.).
Assign (v.) Give a particular piece of work, for example, to a particular person.
Attitude (n.) The position of the aircraft relative to normal, i.e. nose up/down, left/right wing high.
Authorise (v.) To give permission.

Baggage (n.) The suitcases etc. that passengers take with them. Usage is 'standard airline' and American English.
Bassinet (n.) American English for cot (q.v.).
Board (v.) To go onto an aircraft. Also, 'on board' = 'in the aircraft'.
Boarding card/pass (n.) Card issued at check-in desk, usually showing the passenger's seat number, which authorises boarding the appropriate flight.
Brace (v.) Stiffen one's body.
Brief (v.) To give relevant information. Hence *briefing* (n.)
Bulkhead (n.) Internal wall of an airliner.

CA (n.) *See* cabin attendant.
Cabin (n.) The part of an airliner in which the passengers are seated.
Cabin attendant (n.) Member of the cabin crew.
Cabin crew (n.) Those members of an airline's staff who work in the cabin of an airliner.
Cabin pressure (n.) The air pressure inside the cabin. At higher flight levels it is maintained at a pressure higher than that of the air outside the aircraft.
Call button (n.) Button which a passenger may press to call for assistance from a CA.
Cancel (v.) Stop or withdraw from service, with no plan to operate at a later time. Hence *cancellation* (n.).

Captain (n.)
1. The pilot who has full responsibility for the particular flight. He sits in the left-hand pilot's seat.
2. The higher of the two ranks held by airline pilots.

Carrier (n.) An airline in this context.
Cart (n.) American English for trolley (q.v.).
Checklist (n.) A standardised printed list used for regular checks of equipment.
Chute (n.) An inflatable rubber slide, positioned beneath or on an external door, for emergency evacuation.
CIP (n.) Commercially important person. Such persons receive special care from cabin crew because they are commercially important to the airline.
Complimentary (adj.) Free, without charge.
Comply with (v.) Keep to, for example, rules and regulations.
Configuration (n.) Arrangement, for example, of seats.
Co-pilot (n.) The number two pilot on a particular flight. The co-pilot may hold the rank of captain or first officer. The co-pilot sits in the right-hand pilot's seat.
Cot (n.) Small movable bed for a baby, which can be attached to a cabin bulkhead. British English for bassinet.
Crew (n.) Group of people who work together. Usage can be either collective or singular.
Customs (n.) Government department responsible for monitoring the movements of goods into a country and collecting duty (tax) on certain goods.

Declare (v.)
1. Make a decision and announce it as in, for example, declare an emergency.
2. State to a customs officer which goods that are liable for duty are being carried.

Delay
(v.) Make late, reschedule at a later time, e.g. departure has been delayed by 15 minutes.
(n.) The amount of lateness as a length of time, e.g. there will be delay of 15 minutes.
Departure (n.) The act of leaving. (From the verb 'depart'.)
Departure lounge (n.) The room in which passengers wait immediately before boarding an airliner.
Depressurisation (n.) An emergency situation in which cabin pressure drops very rapidly to the level of the outside air.
Descent (n.) Slow, steady, planned downward movement of an aircraft. Also descend (v.)
Designate (v.) Give an official status to.
Deteriorate (v.) Get worse, as in, for example, deteriorating weather conditions.
Disembark (v.) Leave an airliner normally upon arrival. Hence *disembarkation* (n.).
Ditch (v.) Make a forced landing (q.v.) on water. Hence *ditching* (n.).
Dive
(n.) Very rapid downward movement of an aircraft. Such a movement in an airliner is only made in an emergency.
(v.) To perform a dive.
Divert (v.) Fly to an airport other than that planned as the destination. Hence *diversion* (n.).
Drugs kit (n.) Large box containing a wide range of medicines and simple medical equipment for use in an emergency by qualified personnel.
Duty (n.)
1. Piece of work that needs to be done.
2. Tax collected by customs officers on certain goods brought into a country.
3. On duty = working. Off duty = not working.

Economy class (n.) The cheapest class for passengers. Designated by the letter 'Y' on a ticket.
Embark (v.) Board an airliner. Hence *embarkation* (n.).

Emergency (n.) Unexpected and dangerous situation.
Emergency exit (n.) Doorway of an airliner used in an emergency evacuation.
Entrée (n.) In American English and, increasingly, in British English, the main dish of a meal.
Escape chute (n.) *See* chute.
Evacuate (v.) Rapidly leave the airliner in an orderly manner, followed a declared emergency. Hence *evacuation* (n.).
Expedite (v.) Hurry up.
Extinguish (v.) Put out, for example, a cigarette or a fire.
Extinguisher (n.) Piece of equipment containing chemicals for extinguishing (q.v.) fires.

File (n.) Row of people, one behind the other.
Single file: in one column.
Double file: in two columns.
File (v.) Hand in. For example, file a report.
Film (n.) British English for movie.
Final approach (n.) Last 4 miles of an approach (q.v.) in which the airliner is in direct line with the runway for landing.
First aid (n.) Medical help given immediately after an accident of any sort.
First officer (n.) Lower of the two ranks held by airline pilots.
Flight attendant (n.) American English for cabin attendant.
Flight crew (n.) The team of people who fly an airliner.
Flight (n.)
1. Act of flying.
2. Particular journey by air.
Flight deck (n.) The part of the airliner where the flight crew work.
Flight engineer (n.) Member of some flight crews who monitors the state of the aircraft's engines and other systems.
Flight plan (n.) Very detailed form which the captain completes before a flight, giving exact information regarding the intended flight.
Forced landing (n.) Unscheduled landing in an emergency situation.

Galley (n.) Kitchen area of the cabin.
Gasper air outlet (n.) Part of the air conditioning system individually controlled by passengers by adjusting the nozzle (q.v.).
Ground services (n.) Airline division responsible for all airline activities at an airport, except engineering.

Hand baggage (n.) Baggage carried into the cabin by a passenger.
Head-wind (n.) Wind in the opposite direction to the one in which the aircraft is flying. It therefore hinders the aircraft and makes the flight longer. Opposite of 'tail-wind'.

ICAO (n.) *See* International Civil Aviation Organisation.
Immigration (n.) Government department responsible for monitoring the movement of people into a country.
Impact (n.) Collision, crash.
Independent (adj.) Free-standing, e.g. independent oxygen masks which can be used freely throughout the cabin.
Inflate (v.) Fill with air. Hence *inflatable* (adj.).
In-flight magazine Magazine published by an airline and given free to its passengers.
Initiate (v.) Begin, start.
International Civil Aviation Organisation (n.) Agency of the United Nations Organisation responsible for civil aviation. Its particular interests are safety and training standards.

Glossary

Interphone (n.) Airliner's internal telephone system, connecting the flight deck and the cabin.
Irregularity (n.) Something which is not right, discovered, for example, during a check.

Jump seat (n.) Seat which folds away when not in use.

Land (v.) Return to the ground. Hence *landing* (n.).
Landing (n.) Action of returning to the ground. From land (v.)
Leg (n.) A flight with, say, two intermediate stops is said to consist of three legs. For example, a flight from London to Sydney might consist of a London–Bahrain leg, a Bahrain–Singapore leg and a Singapore–Sydney leg.
Liaise (v.) Regularly exchange information with, and discuss matters with, someone else.
Life jacket (n.) Public (i.e. general English) word for life vest (q.v.).
Life raft (n.) Inflatable boat for use after ditching.
Life vest (n.) Inflatable vest which keeps a person afloat in water.
Line up (v.) Turn an aircraft, at the end of a runway, to the direction of the runway ready for take-off.
Luggage (n.) British English for baggage.

Mask (n.) *See* oxygen mask.
Monitor (v.) Watch in order to check.
Movie (n.) American English for film.

Nose (n.) Front of an aircraft.
Nozzle (n.) Controllable outlet of the air-conditioning system.
Nursing mother (n.) In this context, a mother travelling with a young baby.

Operator (n.) In this context, an airline.
Operational difficulties (n.) Literally, problems disrupting normal working. When used as an explanation for, for example, a delay, the expression is therefore meaningless.
Operations room (n.) Room at an airport at which pilots receive the latest weather information and forecasts etc.
Orderly (adj.) In a calm and controlled manner, without panic.
Oxygen mask (n.) Emergency oxygen source, used following depressurisation.

PA (n.) *See* public address.
Passenger service unit (n.) Set of controls above a group of two or three seats, consisting of call button (q.v.). Passenger reading light and gasper air outlet (q.v.).
Patient (n.) Person needing medical help.
Patrol (v.) To walk up and down checking that everything is in order.
PAX (n.) Airline term for passengers.
Pilot (n.) Person trained and qualified to fly an aircraft.
Pitch (n.) The distance between the back of a row of seats and the front of the row behind.
Pneumatic (adj.) A pneumatic headset is one in which the source of the sound is a small loudspeaker in the arm-rest. The headset is therefore non-electrical, being basically just a plastic tube to pass the sound vibrations to the ear from the arm-rest.
PSP (n.) See pre-selected passenger.
Pre-board Board an aircraft before the main group of passengers.
Pre-selected passenger (n.) Before a forced landing, certain passengers are chosen, or pre-selected, to help with the evacuation of the aircraft.
Procedure (n.) Standardised way of doing something.
Public address (n.) Microphone and loudspeaker system.
Purser (n.) Senior member of the cabin crew.
Push back (v.) To move, of an aircraft, backwards and away from the terminal building. Also used as a noun.

Rack (n.) Overhead place for stowage of light baggage, running the length of the cabin above the windows.
Ramp (n.) *See* apron.
Regulations (n.) Official rules.
Row (n.) Series of seats running across the cabin. Rows are indicated by a number, the individual seats by a letter.
Runway (n.) Long straight surface used by an aircraft for take-off (q.v.) and landing (q.v.).

Schedule (n.) Timetable, planned timings of a flight. Flights are said to be ahead of schedule (running early), on schedule (running on time) or behind schedule (running late).
Seal (n.) Official sign, usually made of metal or plastic, to show that some piece of equipment has not yet been used (e.g. fire extinguisher) or is out of use (e.g. bar store). Also used as a verb.
Seatbelt (n.) Adjustable strap used to prevent a passenger being thrown out of his/her seat.
Slide (n.) *See* chute.
Stow (v.) Place baggage etc. away safely. Hence *stowage* (n.).
Stretcher (n.) Portable light-weight bed used for carrying passengers unable to walk.
System (n.) Set of equipment used in an integrated way for a common purpose. For example, electrical system, air-conditioning system, hydraulic system, fuel system.

Tag (n.) Small piece of metal, plastic or cloth attached to something (a) so that it can be pulled or (b) for identification.
Tail (n.) The rear of the aircraft.
Tail-wind (n.) Wind in the same direction as the one in which the aircraft is flying. It therefore helps the aircraft and makes the flight shorter. Opposite of 'head-wind'.
Take off (v.) To leave the ground. Hence *take-off* (n.).
Tariff (n.) List of prices.
Taxi (v.) Of an aircraft, to move along the ground under its own power. Hence *taxying*.
Terminal (building) (n.) Building at an airport used by arriving and departing passengers.
Toggle (n.) *See* tag.
Traffic (n.) The large-scale movement of a number of aircraft.
Trolley (n.) Movable store, pushed along the aisles, containing food, drink or sales stock. In American English, cart.
Turbulence (n.) Sudden change in the flow of air.

UM (n.) (pron. you em) Unaccompanied minor, a child travelling alone for whom the airline has accepted responsibility.
UNMIN (n.) (pron. un-min) Variant of UM (q.v.).

VIP (n.) Very important person; in other words, someone famous.

Wheelchair (n.) Chair mounted on wheels used by passenger unable to walk but otherwise able-bodied.